Clear, Calm and Confident

How To Change Your Life In 30 Days

PENDULUM

First published in 2013
by Pendulum Books

www.pendulum-books.com

SECOND EDITION

ISBN 978 0 9566801 1 2

Cover image © Can Stock Photo Inc. / Jezper

Foreword

I can imagine the excitement and relief that will be felt by readers who are suffering from the 'slings and arrows' of stress when they realise help is at hand.

This is a beautifully designed book. It is very simple, as therapy should be, and yet presents the cutting edge of what psychotherapy research and neuroscience informs us. The explanations of how our brains work are gloriously erudite. Having this understanding would make it difficult for any sufferer not to be able to make better choices in life.

In effect Christian says loud and clear 'this is what works so let's get on with it'. At the same time though he makes it clear that some hard work could be involved.

The brain is essentially a 'pattern matching organism'. A pervading theme in the book is the fascinating case history illustrations that many of us can relate to.

Not only is 'Clear, Calm and Confident' going to be enormously helpful to the public at large but it is also written with the Solution Focused practitioner in mind. As Christian says: 'If you want to take your progress to another level, I highly recommend having a talk to a Solution Focused Hypnotherapist'.

Christian is in some ways a rare commodity. He is a very successful Solution Focused Hypnotherapist who practices what he preaches. Everyone who has the opportunity to come across him either by way of his consulting room or his book is fortunate indeed.

David Newton
DHP FAPHP MNCH MNCP SHS SQHP Sup
Chairman, Association for Solution Focused Hypnotherapists

1

Acknowledgements

My deepest gratitude to my teacher, David Newton at the Clifton Practice in Bristol, whose tireless commitment to teaching and the pursuit of excellence has changed my life and so many others in a profoundly positive way. Thank you to Susan Rodrigues for your guiding hand and supervision. To Lama Jampa Thaye, my teacher on the path, my deepest respect. Thank you to Alison Paine who gave me detailed comments on the manuscript. To my wife, Emily, I am eternally grateful for your creativity, your tireless editing, and your patience.

This book is dedicated to the reader, and to all those I've had the privilege to meet through my clinic. To all of you who commit to making positive changes in your life, thank you, the ripples spread to all our lives... well done, keep going.

Christian Dunham
DHP HPD MNCH (Reg) AfSFH Sup (Hyp)
Senior Lecturer CPHT

About The Author

Christian Dunham has an unusual background for a Solution Focused Hypnotherapist. A professional bass player for over 30 years, he moved to the UK from Australia following a tour with American legend Don McLean. Tired of life on the road and wanting a more fulfilling career than the music business, Christian first decided to train as a Bowen Therapist.

As an Australian, it was a natural choice of therapy. Tom Bowen developed his powerful hands-on remedial technique in Australia in the 1950s to help people suffering from chronic pain, sports injuries and stress-related illnesses. Christian trained at the renowned European College of Bowen Studies and soon found himself inundated by people wanting his help.

Soon after establishing his Bowen practice, he began to realise that stress and anxiety were playing a key role in many of his clients who were presenting physical symptoms of chronic pain and fatigue. He became intrigued by the possibility of treating the body through treating the mind.

Christian decided to train as a Clinical Hypnotherapist and gained his Diploma in Solution Focused Hypnotherapy and Psychotherapy at the prestigious Clifton Practice in Bristol. He also holds the nationally accredited Hypnotherapy Practitioners Diploma - the 'Gold Standard' in Hypnotherapy training - awarded through The National Council For Hypnotherapy.

Christian established a busy practice in the city of Bath and in Kensington, London before relocating back to the Sunshine Coast Hinterland, Australia in 2019. He continues to treat clients all over the world via Skype. He is a member of the

Association for Solution Focused Hypnotherapists and The National Council for Hypnotherapy.

Christian's former career in the music business has given him a particular insight into the power of confidence. Having performed live on television and played all the major concert halls across the UK, Christian understands the debilitating effect of performance anxiety, and how confidence can change your world.

We all excel, and we can all be happy, when we are feeling clear, calm and confident. The intention of this book is to help you achieve that state of mind.

Downloading The MP3

This book comes with a free MP3 download. Please visit www.christiandunham.net/mp3-downloads to get your copy. If you have any queries at all, please feel free to contact me through the website.

Getting On With It

This book is about getting on with it. Right now you can skip to Day 1 of the workbook, do the simple written exercise and listen to the MP3. Do the same thing tomorrow, the day after, and so on for at least the next 30 days and your life will change. It works!

However, it helps and enhances the experience if we understand *why* what we're doing works, and *how* it works, and so in the pages leading up to the workbook section I've explained the process.

Solution Focused Hypnotherapy

Everything you are about to read and do is based on the techniques I use every day in my work as a Solution Focused Hypnotherapist. Solution Focused Hypnotherapy combines the latest methods of Solution Focused Brief Therapy with Clinical Hypnotherapy to create a powerful modern technique that enables positive change quickly and effectively.

This book and the accompanying MP3 are not intended as a replacement for one-to-one sessions with a qualified Solution Focused Hypnotherapist. They are designed to introduce you to some of the techniques used in the therapy and show just how quickly positive, effective, real change can begin to be experienced in your life.

Some techniques are mentioned in this book that are not explained or included in the exercises. The obvious one is the Miracle Question. This is a powerful process that is a key part of Solution Focused Hypnotherapy and which I believe is best facilitated by a skilled, qualified therapist in one-to-one sessions and not suited to the structure of a self-help book.

The simple journal for recording what has been good about your day, the revision of how the brain works through explanations and other people's stories, and listening to the MP3 are all part of the process of Solution Focused Hypnotherapy.

Hearing It Over And Over

You will notice repetition throughout this book. This is not a mistake. Habits are created through repetition and information is absorbed through constantly revising, going over it again and again, and by hearing the same information explained through different contexts and scenarios. Our brain needs to hear things about 10 or 11 times for that information to become part of our internal library of what we know. So by revising and reminding ourselves of how the brain works and why we think, feel and behave the way we do, we truly understand and become conscious of how to use our mind in a positive, creative way.

Just Do It

As I said, habits are created through repetition, just like brushing your teeth, so listening to the MP3 will become a habit. There is no right or wrong way to do this. It really is just a matter of lying down and pressing PLAY. If you drift off in the first 30 seconds that's okay, or if you listen all the way to the end, either way is fine. You will probably find that every time is different. That's okay, it's simply a matter of DOING it.

And finally, all the stories in this book are my first-hand experiences with clients. All the names and identifying details have been changed to protect their confidentiality. As you will see, the powerful, therapeutic results of Solution Focused Hypnotherapy cover a wide range of issues and help to facilitate wonderful changes quickly and effectively.

So now let's get on with it.

Your mind creates your world.

The Buddha

What Is The Brain?

The brain is an immensely powerful, organic, pattern-matching machine. A vast universe of neurons, around 100 billion of them, each neuron connecting through thousands of synapses, 100 trillion connections operating and interacting at speeds and in combinations beyond the comprehension of even the most intelligent of its owners.

As the 'keepers' of this awesomely powerful and amazingly resilient part of our anatomy, we literally owe it to ourselves to understand at least the basics of what we are driving – or what drives us.

I mean, if you discovered that the old Ford that's sitting in your garage was actually a Ferrari, you would at least want to have a look under the bonnet – right?

And if you found that by giving it a bit of a tidy-up, doing a bit of detailing, perhaps changing the oil and water, and maybe giving it a service, it would go further and faster, easily and more efficiently, with no fuss, arriving at destinations you currently only dream of, effortlessly, in what seemed like the blink of an eye?

It would be worth trying, wouldn't it?

Food For Thought

The vast majority of us are very aware of what we put in our bodies. How what we eat affects our physical health and what we can do with our body.

We understand to a reasonably high degree the healthy stuff and the unhealthy stuff. We are constantly bombarded with information about ingredients, new ways to lose weight, programs to get fit, what makes us fat, how smoking causes cancer, about calories, carbs, and endless cooking shows.

Pretty much everything we need to know or want to know about how to live and operate at a physically healthy level of efficiency is available to us at the click of a mouse. It's simply a matter of doing it.

But how many of us know how our brain works? The basic functions in our head that affect our day-to-day lives? How many of us are aware of the constant stream of information going into our mind and how we respond to that information? How wonderful would it be to have control over what we put in our mind just like we have control over what we put in our mouth? To have the resources for positive mental health, to be able to increase our mental fitness, and create the spare capacity in our mind that allows for positive mental behaviour.

The Fast Track To Positive Change

This book is designed to help you achieve just that. It is a fast, effective program that uses the latest understanding of how the brain works alongside the powerful, physical resources available in all of us to initiate profound change in how you think, how you feel and how you behave.

By harnessing the brain's awesome ability to change (called 'neuroplasticity' by neuroscientists), we will strengthen the conscious, intellectual part of the brain, while 'shrinking' down that anxious, negative, limiting part of the brain. In short, changing the way we think, the way we feel and the way we act and behave.

Through changing the neural pathways in our brain, gaining conscious awareness and developing a few simple habits, we can move that 'first response' reaction from the worried, anxious, frustrated part of our brain to the positive, creative part of the brain where we can take control of our lives.

The Easy Way To Happiness

Simply by reading this book, following the simple instructions and listening to the MP3 included with this book you will literally be <u>changing your mind</u>. By combining the methods of conscious awareness, mindfulness, deep relaxation and hypnosis, you are fine-tuning your ability for confidence and happiness in your life. So whether you're cruising along country lanes with the top down and the wind in your hair or flying along the autobahns of this amazing universe with the stereo pumping, it will be yours to choose, yours to enjoy confidently, calmly, always in control.

Now it's simply a matter of doing it!

The Brain: A Short Geography Lesson

If we could open up the lid, disconnect our brain and place it on the table in front of us, our brain would be about the size of a small melon. It weighs around 3lbs or 1.4kg.

We've all seen pictures of the grey matter with that cauliflower-type texture on the top surface. The left side front section of our brain is known as the Left Prefrontal Cortex. If you place your left hand over your forehead above your left eye and sweep it back over your head, that is the area we're talking about.

This is the conscious part of your brain, the part where you know you as 'you'. It's also the creative part of our brain, the part we've been using to dream up and design new ideas and new ways of doing things. From early man innovating tools from stone, from the wheel to WiFi, it all began here. It's the intellectual part of the brain.

This intellectual mind sets us apart from other animals. While other animals may use a stick to poke an anthill for food, they don't fashion tools or innovate means for communication or transport. They don't drive cars or design mobile phones.

The Left Prefrontal Cortex is where we make a proper assessment of situations and come up with solutions. The very fact that you are reading these words is part of a process that began in the intellectual part of your brain. You made an assessment of your situation, your life as it is right now, and decided you were interested in possibly making a few changes.

As you read this book, a few pennies will probably drop and you can then make a decision as to whether you think this program will be a positive way for you to proceed in making those changes – your Left Prefrontal Cortex in action.

Now Let's Look A Bit Deeper

Have you ever wondered where all our anxieties originate? Those fearful, debilitating feelings that limit you, that hold you back? Where is the source of the drip that becomes a trickle that soon turns into a stream before it becomes a flood – a river of tears and depression?

There is another area of the brain known as the primitive part. This area is often referred to as the 'fight or flight' part of the brain. It is located near the physical centre of the brain.

This primitive part of the brain is made up of three bits: the Amygdala, the Hippocampus, and the Hypothalamus. These three parts work together to form a kind of Health and Safety Department. They are always on high alert for anything that might go wrong, that could be a threat, no matter how unlikely. This Health and Safety Department will use up vast amounts of time and energy conjuring up dire situations that will never happen, constantly on high alert just to be sure.

And so as our stress levels rise and our anxiety gradually increases, often without us even noticing in the early stages, we begin to lose intellectual control of our life and slowly we move from the calm, happy, confident, intellectual area of our brain into the primitive area, as the fight or flight part takes over.

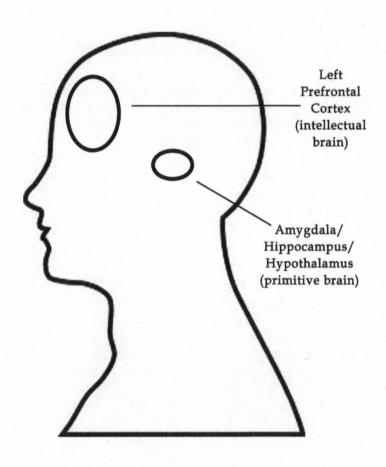

Left
Prefrontal
Cortex
(intellectual
brain)

Amygdala/
Hippocampus/
Hypothalamus
(primitive brain)

The Human Brain

Case History: Amelia

Amelia is 56 years old. She has been suffering chronic physical pain for more than 15 years.

Over this time her tolerance to painkillers has developed to the point where they no longer have any effect. Various alternative therapies promised much but delivered little in the way of relief. So-called Pain Clinics did nothing. The last physiotherapist at her local hospital had discharged her years ago saying there was nothing more that could be done: 'You'll just have to live with it.' Amelia has been self-medicating for the last 10 years.

When we first met, Amelia struggled to get out of the car. Every step caused her pain and climbing the single flight of stairs to my treatment room was a real effort for her.

Amelia rarely left her flat, she had no social life, pain and depression ruled her life. Amelia wanted to be free from the chronic pain and suffering.

Depression, Anxiety And Anger

This primitive part of our brain always operates within the parameters of *depression, anxiety* and *anger*.

These responses have been with us since we were early men and women – they were our defence mechanism against nature and the elements in our daily fight for survival way back in the beginning of time. The battle to stay alive – hundreds of thousands of years of defending ourselves against wild animals, other tribes and the elements – played a big part in forging deep-rooted behaviour patterns and responses in our brain.

When the cold and the dark and the fear all got too much for us, we would have crawled into bed and just wanted to disappear, at least until the sun came out again, much like a modern-day depressive episode.

And just the daily grind of staying alive way back then would have kept us in a constant state of heightened anxiety.

Anger helped us appear stronger and was a very effective defensive tool when faced with threats from wild animals and humans. But these days in our modern world it is not necessary, and quite often inappropriate, to rant and rage against people and situations where we feel we have lost control or we feel threatened.

Case History: Jessica

Maria phoned me in tears. Her daughter Jessica needed help and she didn't know what to do. Someone had given her my number and she had made the call.

Jessica was 21 and had recently passed her driving test. On her first outing she had a minor accident – not her fault – and now she refused to drive ever again. She had low self-esteem and a low body image, seeing herself as fat and ugly. She had hardly any friends, and no social life. She was very anxious about her final university exams that were looming, and... Maria took a deep breath as she began to cry.

'She's cutting herself,' she whispered. 'She hasn't told me but her friend's mother overheard them talking about it and I've seen the marks.'

After a brief conversation reassuring Maria that it was possible to turn this situation around, I said I would be happy to meet with Jessica for a chat if she was willing.

'But she doesn't know I've called you, she doesn't know I know about the self-harming.'

'I won't say a thing about it.'

'She won't want to come, I just know it.'

'Tell her I have some time at 5pm tomorrow,'

'...Yes, but...'

'... And tell her I'm an Australian guy with dreadlocks.'

There was silence for a moment.

'... Right,' said Maria.

Thirty minutes later I received a text: 'Jessica will be there for 5pm tomorrow.'

I wrote the appointment in my diary.

Primitive Brain: Fight Or Flight

Depression, anxiety and anger are all default settings for the primitive fight or flight part of our brain. However, they are not the only telltale signs that we are operating from this part of our brain. This area of our brain is also very negative. It's the bit that is constantly telling us:

'You can't do that.'

'That will never work.'

'Don't bother with that.'

'It's all a bit much.'

'I'm not good enough.'

'What if I fail?'

'What's the point in even trying?'

Primitive Brain: The Health And Safety Officer

Again, I often think of that caricature of the self-important Health and Safety Officer with his uniform and his epaulettes and his cap, with all his keys jangling on his utility belt packed with leather holsters for flashlights and phones and... well you get the picture. That guy at work who won't let you change a light bulb:

'Don't you dare touch that light bulb! You'll fall off that ladder and you'll break your leg, you'll be off work for six months and then you'll sue the company and the company will go broke and then we'll all lose our jobs and thousands of people will be left homeless. And all because you tried to change a light bulb!'

Case History: John

John came to see me suffering from anxiety. He owns a design company that he started from scratch. He started out on his own and now he employs twelve people designing innovative products that sell through major chain outlets. Six or seven years ago he had the world at his feet. The bigger the challenge the more he was up for having a go. As the driving force within the company he was energised and motivated. Now John is not only extremely anxious, he is confused.

'How did I get like this? I didn't see it coming, there was no traumatic event. But now I find myself overwhelmed before I even get out of bed in the morning. I'm waking up in the middle of the night and can't get back to sleep. I've got no energy and when I do get to work I find myself avoiding my colleagues. We have design meetings on Mondays and Wednesdays and I dread them. I used to thrive on the creative ideas we would throw around, the wonderful innovations we would come up with, and the creative challenges we would have to deal with.'

'Now I sit quietly through the meetings, constantly battling with the negative conversations going on my head, hoping nobody can hear my thoughts. This sounds crazy. It actually makes my stomach churn. There I am, surrounded by these creative people with great ideas, and all I can think about is 'That won't work', 'What if it all goes wrong', or 'I can't present that to the client'.'

Not only can John no longer contribute in his design meetings, now he is worrying that everybody is talking about how negative he has become.

Primitive Brain: The Obsessive

This primitive part of our brain is very obsessive. Once it has perceived some kind of threat, sensed a potential danger, it will continue reminding us that the threat is there. It won't let up. In fact it becomes the only thing we can think about. We will be driven to distraction.

For me personally, this characteristic of an obsessive mind takes over when dealing with spiders. I grew up in Australia, a country renowned for its spiders... big ones! Whenever I talk about this obsessive part of the brain I'm reminded of those times back in Australia, sitting engrossed in a television program. I'd get up and go to the kitchen to make toast and milk, and on the way back to the sitting room I'd glance through into one of the other rooms as I passed. More than likely it would be a room I wouldn't need to go into. And there, on the far wall, would be a spider.

It's like a switch is flicked in my mind. All I can think about now is that spider. I get back to the couch and the television but I can't concentrate on the program. I lose interest in the toast and milk. Before I know it I'm back in the hallway peering into that room I don't even need to go into, checking on the spider. I don't even know why I'm looking at it! I don't want it to be there, I'm not going near it! I'm not even going to enter the room... ever.

So then I'm back in front of the TV and all I'm thinking about is the spider so I'm back and forth checking that it's still there... and then I really start to get worried, to feel anxious, even panic a little bit. What if the next time I look the spider isn't there? Oh dear. So back I go again, constantly checking. A totally inconsequential occurrence has become an all-consuming, anxious obsession.

Case History: David

David's sister suggested he call me for a chat. David had been divorced for three years – he'd had a couple of relationships in that time but they hadn't worked out. His temper always got in the way.

'Everything is great for a while and then I start to get these jealous thoughts coming up. I start feeling anxious, worrying about what she's up to. Even when I know there is nothing to worry about.'

David explained that this behaviour had played a big part in his divorce and affected his other relationships. Recently he had started dating someone new and the anxiety and jealousy had started to rear its ugly head again. When they were alone together everything went well. However, social events were more challenging with David obsessing for days about who would be there from his girlfriend's male friends from the past. Add some alcohol to the mix and things could get a bit awkward.

'It feels wonderful when we are together, but it's the constant need for reassurance, the doubts even when she goes to the shop for milk. It's really draining on me and I know how it all ends if I don't sort it out.'

This time David was determined not to mess it up.

Primitive Brain: Hypervigilant

This emotional, primitive brain is very vigilant. Once the warning lights are flashing it starts scanning the horizon looking for more hints of danger, things to be concerned about, reasons to be fearful.

Not only will it check the immediate vicinity, it will trawl through the past reminding us of all the things that might have gone wrong through our lives and it will look around the corner, over the hill and way off into the future to conjure up wild stories and images of potential threats that will never happen. It will even create dangers that don't exist in order to take control of our minds.

Case History: Mary

Mary had always been a very independent woman. She was in her early 40s and the owner of an old and lovingly restored VW Kombi van. Mary spent her summers travelling around the UK going to small festivals and visiting friends.

A few months before she came to see me Mary had started to feel anxious driving on motorways. It wasn't long before she noticed she didn't feel at all comfortable driving on any roads, but it was winter and the roads were icy and she didn't have any plans that required driving. So she parked up the van at home and enjoyed walking to visit friends.

Mary was concerned that she wasn't sleeping as well as she used to and had found herself waking in the middle of the night and eating biscuits with the cup of tea she would make. This was becoming a concern because Mary was putting on weight.

One day as Mary was walking to visit a friend she turned a corner and froze with fear. She had a panic attack. There before her, on the route to her friend's house, was a street of houses with raised front yards, all fronted with gardens supported by retaining walls.

'You'd better not walk past those retaining walls,' the voice in her head warned. 'Those retaining walls can fall down you know. If you happen to be walking past when one of those retaining walls falls down it could kill you.' Mary crossed the road to avoid the row of houses. She began consciously choosing flat routes for the journeys she made around town. The final straw came one day as she rounded a corner and was confronted by retaining walls on both sides of the street.

The voice in her head went into overdrive. Reminding her of all the dangers presented by walking past retaining walls, even creating vague memories of news reports with graphic details of retaining wall tragedies.

'This is crazy,' she thought. 'Those retaining walls are perfectly safe, this is ridiculous.' But that primitive part of her brain was now on high alert, hypervigilant and totally in control of her thoughts, her emotions, and her behaviour. Mary turned and walked home. When she got inside she called me.

Where Does Anxiety Come From?

So where does this anxiety come from? I believe understanding the answer to this question is the key to starting our recovery from anxiety and depression. It should be the most powerful realisation you get from reading this book.

| Anxiety is created by negative thoughts |

The Root Cause Of Anxiety

It is not the events in our life that cause anxiety, it is the thoughts we surround those events with that create anxiety. Once this is understood, change begins very quickly.

You see your thoughts really do create your world. How you think determines how you feel, and how you feel determines how you interact with the world in your day-to-day life.

Case History: Tom

Tom has been suffering from IBS, Irritable Bowel Syndrome, for over 7 years. He has had every test known to medicine. He has had every microscope, camera and scanner inserted into every orifice available.

He has been prescribed drugs to stop him going to the toilet and drugs to get him going again. He has taken sedatives, anti-depressants and even anti-psychotic medication.

On his last visit to his local surgery he was seen by a new doctor. She ordered all the usual tests, again, but she suggested he try something else. She gave him my card and encouraged him to give me a call for a chat.

When we met Tom was quite distressed. He had travelled on public transport as he was no longer confident driving his car. He had been stressed during the entire journey, worried that he might need the toilet and he wouldn't make it in time.

Through the tears and the desperate story of how his life had become a prisoner to bodily functions, we arrived at the moment when I explained how the mind works.

Tom sat bolt upright. I think I actually saw the light bulb go on above his head. His mouth opened but he couldn't speak. He tapped the piece of paper where I had just written that brief sentence: 'It is not the events in our life that cause anxiety, it is the thoughts we surround those events with that create anxiety.'

'That's it,' he said. 'I've always wondered why when I was teaching computer programming at college I never had an IBS attack. I could go all day and not even think about it. I guess I was so engrossed in the problem-solving part of my brain, my intellectual brain.'

'It was only really the last year of teaching, when they started making people redundant, that I started to feel unwell. It was when I started to think I might be next for the sack and all the terrible things that would come with unemployment that my stomach started to really churn. And then it all really kicked off when they let me go, and I've been feeling ill ever since.'

Your Mind Creates Your World

Life is a series of moments all joined together. How we choose to think in each of those moments determines how we feel, and how we feel determines how we behave.

If we choose to think from that part of our brain where we are in control of our thoughts, seeing things for what they really are, we feel calm and relaxed and generally quite happy. That's when we act in that confident, self-assured way and not much really bothers us.

It is when we are operating from the primitive, negative part of our brain that we feel out of control, worried and anxious about everything, fearful, limiting ourselves, constantly dragging up the past and frightened of the future.

We drag those fears and that negativity into the future, constantly reacting to situations rather than being in control of our response to the stream of events that make up our day-to-day life. We know that retaining walls don't cause anxiety, we know that travelling on public transport doesn't cause uncontrollable bowel movements, that driving a car doesn't cause debilitating anxiety.

Millions of people are driving cars right now as you read this book. Happily travelling on motorways, stuck in traffic, having conversations, listening to music. Some are concentrating on what they're doing, others aren't, and most are totally oblivious to the journey they are taking. Driving on motorways, taking public transport, walking past retaining walls are all simply events.

It is not the events in our lives that cause us anxiety, it is the negative thoughts with which we surround these events that create anxiety.

Case History: Kylie (1)

Kylie is a family doctor. She came to see me suffering with insomnia. Kylie had a very disrupted sleep pattern. She found it difficult to get to sleep and when she did finally get to sleep she would wake very abruptly at 2:30am every night. She would be wide-awake and very agitated.

Kylie would get out of bed and wander around the house. She would read, surf the internet, make cups of tea, before finally going back to bed to doze restlessly, eventually rising again around 7am exhausted and very negative about the day, already anxious about the likelihood of the same thing happening again the following night.

Kylie had a lot of stress in her life. She loved her job and had a very compassionate interest in the welfare of her patients but she wasn't happy in the work environment of the surgery where she worked. The 'office politics' were getting her down.

Kylie's husband travelled with his work, so often he was away all week. Through all of this her mother was suffering with a long-term illness and Kylie was caring for her at home. She described the constant stream of thoughts that poured through her mind, thoughts of worry and negativity.

The stress of her day-to-day responsibilities ran like an endless loop in her head and then at night those same thoughts ran wild into the future. Exhausting visions of her life out of control and nothing ever changing.

The Stress Bucket

All our negative thoughts are collected and accumulated. We say we store them in our 'stress bucket'. Every day of our lives, over the weeks and months and years, we've been stashing away our stress and our negativity in that stress bucket. We pour it in there and it builds up until it's flowing over the top and all that negativity and stress is spilling out all over the place, creating quite a mess.

Emptying The Stress Bucket: REM

Fortunately our body has a wonderful method for emptying our stress bucket. It's called REM sleep. REM stands for Rapid Eye Movement.

In his book 'The Users Guide To The Brain' (p.134), John Ratey MD, associate clinical professor in psychiatry at Harvard University, explains how during REM sleep a host of neurons, operating on autopilot and less constrained due to sleep, create the imagery of both clear dreams and metaphorical fantasy dreams. These fantastic images and stories occur during REM sleep and this is how our brain works to make sense of and take control of our previous day's experiences.

During our REM sleep we move the previous day's experiences from the primitive, emotional part of our brain into the intellectual Left Prefrontal Cortex area of our brain where we have control over these memories.

When we have uninterrupted sleep we wake up feeling calm and refreshed. So often some event that may have troubled us during the day before, perhaps really got inside our head and annoyed us for the rest of the day and even into the evening, has now been completely forgotten or it just doesn't matter anymore. We wake feeling energised, positive and motivated. This is thanks to REM sleep. REM is how we empty that stress bucket.

REM sleep makes up about 20% of our average nightly sleep pattern and we don't get any overtime out of it. So even if it is only a quarter of the way into its job of ploughing through our stored up stress and anxiety and REM time gets called, our REM sleep finishes and that's when we wake up, often abruptly with a start, feeling agitated and alert.

Often we can't get back to sleep and we lie there for ages worrying about stuff before perhaps nodding off, finally waking again feeling tired, exhausted and stressed out before our feet have even hit the floor. Our brain uses a lot of energy trying to get back to the REM state that empties that stress bucket.

Introducing The All-Important MP3

That's where the MP3 included with this book comes in. I will explain more about the MP3 later but for now here is a quick introduction.

The MP3 creates a wonderfully calm and deep state of relaxation that helps bring on the REM state. By introducing a relaxed trance state, we use the proven therapeutic power of hypnosis to help the mind let go of stress and to relax. At the same time we begin to create new positive neural pathways in the brain to promote positive mental behaviour.

In their book 'Human Givens' (p.278-279), Joe Griffin and Ivan Tyrrell discuss how: 'When an individual is in REM state new learning can best be programmed.'

They go on to explain how: 'Hypnotic induction works by duplicating part of the REM state... Hypnotic inductions are artificial ways of consciously accessing the REM state. That is why hypnosis is such a powerful psychological tool for raising self-esteem, increasing confidence, helping an individual practice new skills, or improve their social performance.'

Case History: Clifford

Clifford was referred to me by his GP. Clifford was deeply depressed. His depression had been medically diagnosed and he was prescribed sleeping pills and anti-depressants.

Clifford is in his 60s and single. His elderly mother had passed away four months before. Having been his mother's carer for many years and providing palliative care all the way through to the end in his mother's own home, Clifford was struggling with the grief and the loss.

He found getting out of bed difficult – often he didn't even bother. He would stay in bed under the covers in his room all day. Then when he couldn't sleep at night, he would wander around the house, grazing on junk food and drinking tea in front of the television. His daughter would come and visit him during the week, trying unsuccessfully to get him out for a walk to exercise.

As we progressed through our initial consultation I could see Clifford was struggling to engage or to interact with what I was talking about.

He acknowledged his depression and his negativity. He listened to the bit about how anxiety is created through negative thoughts. I think I even saw an eyebrow twitch when I mentioned the stress bucket.

For Clifford the first penny really dropped when I started to explain the physiology of what was happening in his brain. How the chemicals created in our brain affect our state of mind and why anti-depressants are prescribed.

The Brain's Reward System: Serotonin

The brain has a wonderful process for helping us cope with the events in our lives. It gives us rewards for operating effectively as human beings.

These rewards we get are coping mechanisms, which act as motivators. They help us feel calm and confident and brave. They motivate us to rise above adversity, making us feel happy and confident when we do, and promoting the continuation of more of the same behaviour – interacting positively and perpetuating the species. A very important motivation!

The rewards we create in the brain are chemical processes that produce neurotransmitters. These neurotransmitters are the catalyst for positive mental behaviour. The brain produces many different neurotransmitters but the one we focus on is called 'serotonin'.

Serotonin is the most important chemical for creating a happy, confident, coping mind. It makes us feel calm and motivated, it helps us cope with fear and even helps us cope with pain.

Dr. John Ratey describes serotonin as: 'the brain's brake and policeman, it prevents the brain from getting out of control from fear and worry. It has a calming effect that helps us to assure ourselves that we are going to survive. It elevates mood and self-esteem.'

When we are depressed our brain is not producing serotonin. That is why the doctor will prescribe anti-depressants. Through anti-depressant medication they are trying to kick-start the flow of serotonin. At the other end of the scale, when we are anxious, we are producing lots of neurotransmitters - noradrenaline, cortisol, adrenaline - but no serotonin.

As I said earlier, when we are operating from that primitive part of our brain ie. depressed, anxious and negative, we are not producing any serotonin. It is only when we move out of this area and begin functioning from our intellectual brain, the Left Prefrontal Cortex, where we can make a proper assessment of our lives, making the best choices for how we want to live, that we begin the flow of serotonin.

Once we get the flow of serotonin started it becomes self-perpetuating. It promotes more of the behaviour that continues the process of producing serotonin and so we are motivated to do more of the same positive behaviour.

The Serotonin Formula

A simple formula to explain the process of producing serotonin is:

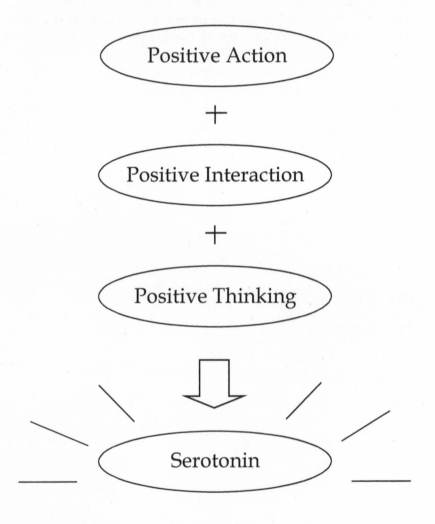

Positive Action

Positive action doesn't have to be major activity. Someone suffering with deep depression is probably not going to race out the door and join a gym. For some it may be a gentle walk in the garden or the park, for others it may be tidying the clothes that have been piling up in the corner of the room, perhaps cleaning the kitchen or even having a shave, vacuuming the house, or maybe finally picking up the phone that has gone unanswered for weeks. This activity may eventually lead to going for a long walk, perhaps a swim at the local pool. Whatever the choices that begin to be made and the decisions taken, the serotonin starts to drip-feed through our brain, motivating us to do more positive actions and positive activities which in turn produce more serotonin.

Positive Interaction

Positive interaction will probably not begin with a weekend of partying across town. However, it could mean a cup of tea with a neighbour, perhaps spending time at the allotments tending the vegetables, or a walk in the countryside communing with nature. Answering the phone can lead to new opportunities for interacting positively. Walking the dog is a wonderful form of positive interaction. You can always borrow one if you don't have your own. This of course leads to interaction with the dog's owners... and the ripples begin to flow.

Positive Thinking

Positive thinking can begin with gratitude, being grateful. Simply taking a moment to acknowledge with gratitude something you appreciate. Writing a short list of the good things about your day – the beautiful sunset, the fact the sun is out, or the much-needed rain. Perhaps appreciating a picture, a piece of music, or a book. The memory of a kind gesture or a friendly smile. Positive thinking begins small and grows very quickly. It can begin with a phone call to a friend to say hi, to say thank you.

Positive thinking is a complementary element of positive action and positive interaction. Positive thinking can become a habit very quickly. The neurons in our brain are very fluid and we can create new thought processes, new neural pathways that become our default method of thinking simply through practicing very easy exercises. One very powerful exercise that quickly becomes a habit and utilises the 'neuroplasticity' of the brain is included in the workbook section of this book.

Case History: Kylie (2)

For Kylie the pennies dropped throughout our initial consultation. She could see very clearly the relationship between the stresses in her life and her sleep problems.

Over the next few weeks she listened to the MP3 every night and very quickly her sleep patterns returned to normal – she was sleeping right through the night and waking feeling refreshed and motivated in the morning.

This positive start to her day gave her the confidence to take control of the other areas of her life that were causing her stress and anxiety. Within six weeks she had left her job at the clinic and started a new job as a locum doctor where not only did she have more freedom and control over her hours, but her income increased.

With this new control over her time and her income she had more resources to help care for her mother and spend time with her husband. Increased energy, increased confidence, motivated and in control of her life with more resources available for the people she loves and her patients – fantastic!

Mighty oaks from little acorns grow.

Old English proverb

A Note About Neuroplasticity

'How do we regulate our emotions? The answer is surprisingly simple - by thinking about them. The Prefrontal Cortex allows each one of us to contemplate his or her own mind... we know when we are angry, every emotional state comes with self-awareness attached, so an individual can try to figure out why he's feeling what he is feeling.' (Jonah Lehrer).

This book is written with the specific intent of offering a practical program to facilitate positive change quickly... a 'let's get on with it' approach. However, a simple understanding of some of the latest scientific discoveries can only help to enhance the effectiveness of the program.

You *Can* Teach An Old Dog New Tricks

My grandfather lived to the ripe old age of 101. His mantra for the last 40 years of his life after he retired was: 'You can't teach an old dog new tricks'. When I suggested he get a mobile phone: 'You can't teach an old dog new tricks'. I got the same response when I offered him a DVD player, even though 20 years earlier he had come to terms with a VCR machine.

Until very recently 'you can't teach an old dog new tricks' was how we assumed the brain worked. Now, through quantum advances in science and technology, the paradigm-busting understanding of 'neuroplasticity' has stood the 'old dog/new tricks' theory on its head. The well-worn arguments of 'I'm too old to learn another language', 'I'm too old to learn how to use a computer', 'I wish I had learned to play the piano when I was younger', have now been completely neutralised.

The Brain's Ability To Change

Neuroplasticity is the term we use to describe the brain's ability to change. It is the brain's physical capacity to create new neural pathways - recycling neurons and creating new connections between those neurons to change the way we think, the way we feel, and the way we behave.

While my grandfather bought into that old mindset of old dogs and new tricks, my mother was the complete opposite. She had always wanted to play the piano so at 65 years of age she finally had her first piano lesson. She loved it and she kept the lessons up. Along the way she ditched the old beat-up piano a friend had resurrected for her, and she bought a lovely new piano... it was in tune and all the keys worked! Now in her mid-70s, my mum still plays the piano every day, still amazed at how wonderful the theme tune from the film 'Titanic' sounds when it's played in tune.

The truly wonderful thing about this story is not only did it prove to her that she could do it, it inspired something else. She realised she could achieve unfulfilled goals, she could learn new things... and she got MOTIVATED.

The next goal my mum set herself was to study. She had always loved painting and drawing and she began to look around for courses in art. Living on her farm in rural Australia meant access to these courses was a challenge. Rising to the challenge, she bought herself a laptop and set about learning how to use the internet. Of course this opened up new possibilities and new opportunities, and all along the way she was developing new resources and discovering new capabilities.

As these new capacities grew, so her confidence increased. Finally my mother settled on a Bachelor of Fine Art degree course. As of writing this, my 73-year-old mother is three years into her Bachelor of Arts degree.

What began with a piano lesson, a desire to fulfil an unrealised ambition led her down a new path. A path that physically changed her brain and her life completely.

Neuroscience And The Dalai Lama

His Holiness The Dalai Lama, Tibetan Buddhism's spiritual leader, is a very logical man. He has supported and encouraged scientific exploration of the brain and encourages research into the mind. Tibetan Buddhism and the practice of the Buddhist path, known as Dharma, place a lot of emphasis on understanding and controlling the mind. In-depth neuroscientific analysis has been conducted on the brain physiology and activity of Tibetan monks. Scans show that the physical size of the Left Prefrontal Cortex of their brains is actually larger than the average human being.

There is clear scientific evidence that through understanding how our brain works, using techniques of meditation and visualization, and harnessing the power of hypnosis using positive metaphor and relaxation, we can create physical changes in our brain that manifest themselves as happiness and confidence in our day-to-day reality... our life.

The Desire For Change

Just as we can take measures to lower our cholesterol, strengthen our muscles and decrease our weight, so we can intervene to lower our anxiety, increase our confidence and lift depression.

We are all hardwired for happiness. We revel in it when we are happy and energised, and search for it when we are not. It is that desire to be relieved of suffering that is the common denominator in every person I see in my clinic. The desire for change, to lift themselves out of the situation they've found themselves in, to rise above those limiting conditions. It is that will and determination that leads inevitably to success and happiness.

Success is getting what you want.
Happiness is wanting what you get.

Dale Carnegie

The Process

The exercises in this book take about 30 minutes every day. The first part is writing down a simple list of the good things that have happened during the day. In a clinical session this is exactly how we begin each session.

I ask the question 'What's been good about your week?' and we write down a list. This is important. It begins the process of creating new neural pathways in your brain. For you to recall the memories of the good things that happened in your day you have to think from the Left Prefrontal Cortex of your brain. That's where those memories are stored. It's a bit like lifting a weight at the gym. When we start we pick up the lightest dumbbell and can only do a few repetitions – and initially you may only find two or three good things about your day. However, it doesn't take long for us to be picking up the bigger weights and doing more repetitions. Before long we start running out of space on the page to list all the good things in our day.

'What's Been Good About Your Day?'

Remember, it's the little things that count: 'I saw a beautiful sunset on Tuesday', 'I said good morning to someone at the bus stop this morning', 'An old friend called for a chat', 'I rang my sister', 'I noticed the leaves falling from the trees', 'My husband did the dishes'.

It's those positive events in our day that we become conscious and mindful of that act as the weights and repetitions for our brain as we create and strengthen new neural pathways. This repetition of recalling positive memories – 'What's been good about your day?' – literally changes the physical structure of the brain.

Now Press 'Play'

The next step, immediately after writing out your list, involves deep relaxation using the MP3 included in this book. The deep levels of relaxation experienced while listening to the MP3 bring on the REM state which helps empty our stress bucket. Emptying the stress bucket allows us to get back to positive, healthy sleep patterns, and wake feeling energised and motivated.

Through REM we lower our anxiety by reducing the negativity we pour into our brains and increasing the spare capacity in our minds for positivity. And of course when we are positive and energised we are more active, interacting positively with the world around us, thinking more positively and generating that serotonin neurotransmitter which makes us calm, brave, motivated, coping and relaxed about our lives. Spending even more time in our intellectual brain, the Left Prefrontal Cortex, where we feel positive, and creative and calm.

So at the end of every day make that list: 'What's been good about your day?' Then lie down somewhere quiet and comfortable and listen to the MP3. Simply pressing PLAY is all you have to do. Relax and allow the words and the music to wash over you. There is no need to concentrate – if you fall asleep that's okay. My voice will count you back to full wakefulness at the end.

The gentle music and my relaxing words will have a calming, hypnotic effect that soothes your mind, allowing your subconscious and your conscious minds to come into balance, relaxing you more and more. These gentle thoughts will have a very positive effect that builds and grows stronger the more you use the MP3.

Habits are created through repetition and the positive effects of this program are enhanced the more you participate. The more often you do it, the more powerful the results. Do this every day for 30 days and you will see your whole world change. And the MP3 will become a positive, effective resource that you can continue to use.

Your thoughts create your world. As your thoughts begin to change, your life begins to change – for the better.

What's Been Good About Your Day?

Write down a list of 3 things that have been GOOD about your day, no matter how small or insignificant you might think them to be. Feel free to write more if you want to.

1. _____

   _____

2. _____

   _____

3. _____

   _____

Now listen to the MP3.

Case History: Tom

Tom was studying when we first met. He was training in a specialised form of teaching – this meant working in school during the day and studying in the evening. He was feeling anxious about his exams that were coming up in a few months.

Tom had never had a 'comfortable' relationship with the headmistress at the school. As one of the few men in his chosen profession, he felt his boss was constantly on his case, overbearing, and this increased his anxiety. He often felt like a 'rabbit caught in the headlights'. He knew intellectually what he should be doing at work but felt uncertain and insecure when it came to the moment of decision. Tom was having trouble utilising the initiative he knew he had.

Tom had travelled the world in-between his last job and taking up his current training. He knew he had been confident in the past and the anxiety about losing his confidence felt like an ever-diminishing spiral, a loop he couldn't get out of.

In our first session I asked Tom, on a scale of 1 to 10, where his confidence was. He said he was about 6/10. I then asked him what would be different in the week ahead if he was 7/10 confident.

'I have a display to put up in the classroom, so I'd make some creative decisions about that.'

'What else would let you know you had moved up a notch in confidence to 7/10?' I asked.

'I'd get creative and use my initiative and put the display up.'

'And who would notice this small change in your confidence?'

49

'My boss would notice because the display would just be done. And I guess I'd notice. Yeah, I would definitely notice.'

At the next session I asked Tom what had been good about his week.

'I'm enjoying work more, I've noticed I feel quite relaxed in the morning before I leave home... oh and I put that display up. I was thinking about this moment, when you ask me the 'good things' question, as I was building it.'

We laughed.

'So where is your confidence at the moment?' I asked.

'I'd say 7/10,' he said.

'If you woke up tomorrow and small changes were occurring and you felt 8/10 confident, what would let you know you had moved up from 7/10 to 8/10?'

'We have a staff meeting first thing tomorrow and if I was 8/10 confident, I'd be there early, I'd have spare time to feel relaxed and have a cup of coffee.'

'What else would let you know things had subtly shifted up to 8/10 in your day?'

'Well I'd be contributing in the meeting, instead of sitting there with ideas but not saying anything. I'd offer some input into the meeting.'

'And how would you know you were feeling 8/10 confident?'

'I'd be really calm as I spoke. The words would naturally flow... some of my colleagues might even nod their heads in agreement,' he laughed.

At our next session Tom couldn't wait to get to his list of good things in his week.

'I understand my boss a lot better now,' he said. 'She has a lot of responsibility to get me up to the high standard expected of this school. I feel more positive towards her. I also did say a few things at the meeting and I felt better in myself for it. I feel like I was generally much more focused at work this week... oh and I've started study revision which is so not me.'

Over the next few sessions Tom felt his confidence and his happiness gradually increase to 9/10. He noticed his boss compliment him about small things during the day. Tom began applying for jobs for after his exams and he continued his study revision. He felt like he was 'on top of things' for the first time in years.

At our final session Tom said he was feeling 9.5/10 confident and happy. He found he was utilising his training and skills in a way that flowed easily during the day. He was aware that the skills and resources he had been learning were now becoming second nature. He felt ready and prepared for his exams next week. He was also aware that he had been successful in one of his job interviews and that a job was there for him when he passed his exams.

Strangely, he said, this only made him more confident about the exams, whereas in the past it would have added to the pressure and the anxiety. I received an email from Tom a few weeks later. He passed his exams comfortably and after his summer break he was taking up the job offer.

What's Been Good About Your Day?

Write down a list of 3 things that have been GOOD about your day, no matter how small or insignificant you might think them to be. Feel free to write more if you want to.

1. _____

_____

2. _____

_____

3. _____

_____

Now listen to the MP3.

How Your Mind Creates Your World

Everything begins with a thought. A thought creates the feeling and the feeling determines the behaviour pattern or the actions that we take. Our thoughts determine how we interact with the world. So if we have a thought that makes us feel negative or fearful, then we act and behave in a way generated by fear, anger or anxiety. But if we have a thought that we're in control, then we act in a way that takes control of the situation. That's the intellectual mind in action – the creative part, the part that comes up with dreams and ideas about the future, and allows us to put those thoughts into action.

Thoughts are electrical signals travelling at superfast speed along the neural pathways we have built in our brain. Billions of neurons connected in our own unique way passing that electrical spark across the synapses that join each neuron together. As the spark crosses the synapse a neurotransmitter can be triggered. A chemical is released, allowing the neurons to communicate. There are many types of neurotransmitters including noradrenaline, dopamine, and serotonin, to name just a few.

The one we talk about the most is serotonin. Serotonin regulates appetite, sleep, mood and behaviour. It makes us feel calm, relaxed and brave. It also plays a key role in lifting depression. When anti-depressants like Prozac are prescribed, the drug is trying to hold the serotonin in the synapse longer, strengthening the potential for communicating the feeling of calm through the brain. These feelings of calm, triggered by positive thoughts that promote the communication of serotonin through the brain, act as the catalyst for positive mental behaviour that then manifest as our real experience in the world.

If our thoughts stimulate the flow of the neurotransmitter noradrenaline, a stress hormone which triggers the fight or flight response in the Amygdala, increasing blood pressure and ramping up anxiety to keep us on high alert, it is easy to understand how such thoughts create the feelings of stress that make us feel scared and negative, anxious and exhausted.

However, if our thoughts are calm and positive, stimulating a constant steady flow of serotonin through our brain, then we respond to the events of our day in a relaxed and positive way. Our life flows easily and we create a calm, relaxed environment, aware of the good things in our life, constantly maintaining and building the causes and conditions for more of the same.

What's Been Good About Your Day?

Write down a list of 3 things that have been GOOD about your day, no matter how small or insignificant you might think them to be. Feel free to write more if you want to.

1. _____

   _____

2. _____

   _____

3. _____

   _____

Now listen to the MP3.

Case History: Kelly

Kelly was grieving over a relationship. She was struggling with her broken heart and finding it very difficult to deal with her future. Kelly over-analysed everything and said she was going over and over her break-up in her mind. Constantly going round in circles, obsessing about it. She said she really needed to get grounded and start moving forward with her life.

At our first session Kelly said her happiness was a 2/10. I asked her the Miracle Question: what would be different about the week ahead if a miracle occurred and she felt happier? Kelly replied that she would phone her best friend and meet for lunch.

Over the next few weeks Kelly started sleeping better, her energy levels increased and she started doing things for herself again.

On her sixth session Kelly bounced into my room, very happy and full of energy.

'What's been good about your week?' I asked.

'That CD,' she said, 'that CD is doing some weird stuff.'

'Okay... what exactly?'

'Well, I listen to it every night and I've got to say I've never slept better. It really is emptying that stress bucket. I get to the bottom of those stairs and I'm gone. But this week I'm sure I've heard some new stuff on it. It's like you've added new bits to it. Now I know you haven't, it's the same CD, but I've been listening to that CD for about six weeks now and I swear I heard some new things on it this week.'

We laughed about it and I congratulated her on listening to the CD every night. I explained how as the subconscious mind and the conscious mind start working together co-operating and communicating, the mind focuses on new phrases and information. I assured her I wasn't sneaking round to my clients' houses switching CDs.

What's Been Good About Your Day?

Write down a list of 3 things that have been GOOD about your day, no matter how small or insignificant you might think them to be. Feel free to write more if you want to.

1. _____

_____

2. _____

_____

3. _____

_____

Now listen to the MP3.

The Brain's Amazing Ability To Change

Neuroplasticity is the term we use for the brain's ability to change. The actual physiology of the brain is constantly in a state of flux – brain cells are constantly being adapted to new processes as we learn new things.

Just as when you're a child you learnt how to play the piano or the violin and maybe you stuck with it because your parents made you. Then, as you move into your teens, you don't want to do that anymore, so you get into computers, or photography, or football, or some other interest. The brain will utilise those neurons and those neural pathways that were used for playing the piano or the violin and it will start applying them – recycling them in a sense – to use them for these new interests.

Neuroplasticity is that ability of the brain to pick up and implement new ideas and practically apply them in our life. Just like in some people's lifetimes mobile phones and computers didn't even exist, now their brain has applied its ability for change to allow them to learn how to use those new technologies.

These techniques that you're practising now – reminding yourself what's been good about your day, and listening to the MP3 – are literally changing the physiology in your brain.

It can be described this way: throughout your life, you've been getting up each day and going to work the same way, having the same thoughts, doing the same things, responding the same way to different situations. Sometimes it doesn't even make any sense but it's always the same end result. It's a bit like getting up in the morning and going to work down the same road that's got a big hole in the middle of it and every day you fall in the same hole.

What you are doing now is building a new pathway. You are literally building a new pathway of neurons. By being aware of the positive things in your life, you begin to function from that intellectual part of your brain, creating new strands of neurons which work together to create a new path.

So now when you go to work every day, you're walking down that new path. As you practise walking that new path it gets clearer and clearer, more and more defined, more comfortable, and it turns into a nice broad sidewalk. Then it turns into a nice big road, then it turns into a big smooth highway and that old path with that big hole in it is slowly growing over, it's disappearing back into the vegetation and after a while that old path isn't there anymore. You can't find it, you can't see it, because you're so focused on this wonderful new path that you've created – no holes, no overgrowth. It's a very clear, easy path.

Now you are taking control. You are doing this physically in your brain. You are creating new neural pathways, and you do it by practicing – by the repetition of thinking positively, feeling positive, and then acting and behaving in a positive way.

What's Been Good About Your Day?

Write down a list of 3 things that have been GOOD about your day, no matter how small or insignificant you might think them to be. Feel free to write more if you want to.

1. _____

_____

2. _____

_____

3. _____

_____

Now listen to the MP3.

Case History: Phil

Phil is a professional musician. He plays the cello in a string quartet. Phil was suffering from debilitating anxiety when we first met. He has exceptional talent and was destined for great things in his music career by the time he finished high school.

Now in his late 20s, Phil's own assessment of his life is 'wasted'. He teaches the basic grades to schoolchildren during the week and on the weekend the quartet play at weddings. He goes to sleep late, spending hours just surfing the internet, he smokes cigarettes, 'far too much dope', and is putting on weight. At home he is depressed, when playing music he is anxious. Phil rated his happiness level at about 3 or 4 out of 10.

When I first asked Phil the Miracle Question ('Imagine a magic wand was waved tonight while you slept. When you wake tomorrow what small change would be happening to let you know that a miracle had occurred?'), he said he would go out with his mate Rick for a beer after work. That would be a 5/10 week for him.

Over the next few weeks Phil did go out with Rick for that drink. He also started sleeping better, spending less time on the net. He said he had cut back on the dope also.

At our fourth session, Phil was feeling 7/10 happy and confident. I asked him what was good about his week and he said he had started practicing the cello again. Practising like he used to, difficult pieces that challenged him. He'd gone to a party with Rick on the weekend and had actually spoken to people he didn't know and it went well.

When I asked Phil what would be different in the week ahead if he was feeling 8/10 confident, he said he would find a cello teacher who could help him improve his playing.

Over the ensuing weeks Phil's confidence increased, he started sleeping much better, and the dope smoking had gone down to a few joints on the weekend. He was still smoking cigarettes but it was annoying him.

It was our ninth session with Phil feeling 9/10 that he felt a major priority shift. When I asked him what had been good about his week he told me he had rung the Royal Academy in London to enquire about the best cello teacher in his area. He got talking to the person at the Academy and he realised in that moment he really needed and wanted to get back to that higher level of performance and playing ability, to surround himself in music and musicians, to really develop the exceptional talent he had. He asked for the application forms for the Royal Academy to be sent to him and, with consideration of his current circumstances, made a proper assessment of how best to approach studying. Phil committed himself to beginning a full-time Bachelor of Music course at London's Royal Academy in 12 months' time.

Phil also asked me to do a stop-smoking hypnotherapy session the following week. I still see Phil for a few sessions every year – top-ups when new challenges appear in his life. He is studying cello and performing in orchestras. Phil is a non-smoker.

What's Been Good About Your Day?

Write down a list of 3 things that have been GOOD about your day, no matter how small or insignificant you might think them to be. Feel free to write more if you want to.

1. _____

   _____

2. _____

   _____

3. _____

   _____

Now listen to the MP3.

Choosing The Thoughts We Feed Our Mind

Choosing the food we eat has a direct influence on our physical health. 'You are what you eat' is how the saying goes. The size of the portions, the content and quality of the food we eat, the amount of alcohol we consume, whether we choose to smoke – these all have a powerful influence on our physical health and our ability to interact with the world.

These days we are all aware of the impact our eating habits have on our bodies. We have celebrity chefs showing us what is best for us, how to cook, even running television campaigns to change our awareness towards healthy eating. We have fitness DVDs and local gyms offering deals, personal trainers writing columns in newspapers and magazines. We are all aware of the positive and negative consequences of how we treat our body. We all know that what we put in our mouth will determine how our body responds and what the consequences of those actions are.

But very few of us take the time to gain the same awareness of the thoughts we feed our mind. And it's *our* mind, we have a choice – we can choose what thoughts we plant in our mind. We can nurture those thoughts, just like asking you right now to remember that wonderful holiday you had where it was warm and sunny and you were relaxed, feeling care-free, feeling like you were on top of the world. And right now as you recall that memory, you feel better. You go there, you can see it, you can feel it and it makes you feel better. You have just chosen to put that thought in your mind.

We can do that with every thought during our day. As we take control of our thoughts, we get control of the feelings that

70

go with those thoughts, and as we choose to feel in control, choose to feel confident, so we begin to act confidently, and other people perceive us to be confident.

So as we choose the thoughts and the feelings of confidence, of feeling happy and self-assured, we begin to act in a calm, confident way, and as we're seen to be calm and confident, other people respond to us as a calm, confident person, reinforcing the idea in our minds that choosing that thought of being calm and relaxed will help us feel calm and relaxed and so we will act and behave in a calm and relaxed way.

Habits are created through repetition, so as we continue to practise feeling calm and relaxed, we very quickly begin to naturally act in a calm and relaxed way and other people naturally respond to us as a calm and relaxed person. Then our whole world changes very quickly.

So it is very important to pay attention to the thoughts we feed our mind.

What's Been Good About Your Day?

Write down a list of 3 things that have been GOOD about your day, no matter how small or insignificant you might think them to be. Feel free to write more if you want to.

1. _____

_____

2. _____

_____

3. _____

_____

Now listen to the MP3.

Case History: Keith

Keith is in his late 40s. He is married and works in management for a hospital. Keith checks things obsessively. His Obsessive Compulsive Disorder (OCD) is at its worst in the evening. He is in a constant state of anxiety and can be quite confrontational in a defensive, oversensitive way. This agitation is amplified by his debilitating sleep patterns. Keith averages about four hours' sleep every night.

His OCD presents itself at home as worrying about switches, doors, windows, and gas. As it gets closer to bedtime he becomes anxious and starts checking the windows are locked, then the doors, next come the lights and electric switches, finally the gas is checked, then it's back to the windows, doors, etc. By this time his wife is in bed, and as his anxiety grows so does the checking.

OCD is a slippery opponent to tame. We started by creating a regular time to play the MP3 every night. Keith chose 11.30pm and he was very disciplined about going to lie down and listen to the MP3 every night. This gave him an extra half hour of relaxation each night when he started and in the first few weeks occasionally he would allow that to linger before the need to check the gas kicked in.

Over the next few sessions I learnt more about Keith. He had very strict routines about cleaning and cooking. Often he would find himself throwing away bags of unused food when the use-by date had arrived and he hadn't used it. Vacuuming the house was a precision exercise that took days and days of preparation in Keith's head to undertake.

The sixth session with Keith was a breakthrough session. Keith was now getting to bed by 1am and getting about six hours' sleep. I asked him what had been good about his week and he said the strangest thing had happened.

Keith told me he had woken up Saturday morning and he'd slept later than normal. He estimated he'd had about 7½ hours. While he was having his breakfast he said to his wife 'I think I'll wash the car today'. He got up from the table, sorted out the cleaning gear and got on with it. Keith washed the outside and vacuumed the inside. His wife was amazed watching this spontaneous activity. What really left her standing there with mouth agape was when Keith had finished vacuuming the car, he walked into the house, plugged the vacuum cleaner in and began vacuuming the living room. His wife couldn't believe it.

The strange thing for Keith was, it didn't feel strange at all. He said he came into the house with the vacuum cleaner, saw a job that needed doing and just did it. What shocked him was how easy it was to be spontaneous. For the first time he realised how much energy he was using being so tight about everything.

Over the next few weeks Keith reported other changes. He noticed he was buying less at the supermarket and throwing less food out as he became more relaxed about using food. He also used up food by cooking and freezing it to use later, thus wasting less. His sleep settled in at about six hours every night. Some nights he would have to check things a few times before getting to bed, but those times didn't seem like a problem anymore.

What's Been Good About Your Day?

Write down a list of 3 things that have been GOOD about your day, no matter how small or insignificant you might think them to be. Feel free to write more if you want to.

1. _____

   _____

2. _____

   _____

3. _____

   _____

Now listen to the MP3.

The Root Cause Of Anxiety

All anxiety is created from negative thoughts. It's not the events in our life that create anxiety, it's the thoughts we surround those events with.

It's just like the student who has an exam. Exams don't cause anxiety – it's the thoughts that we take into that exam (how we will perform, how much we know and how confident we feel) that create the anxiety. Just like driving down motorways does not cause anxiety – it's the thoughts we surround the act of driving with that create anxiety.

All anxiety is created through negative thoughts so as we take control of our thoughts, feeling positive and calm and relaxed, the anxiety disappears.

Anxiety is one of the default modes of our primitive brain. When we get into that Amygdala, Hippocampus, and Hypothalamus part of our brain, it always defaults to the parameters of depression, anxiety and anger.

When we were primitive men and women, trying to stay alive out on the plains or in the jungles, our finger was pretty much constantly on the panic button, constantly in a state of heightened alert for any danger as we tried to compete with wild animals and other wild tribesmen for survival. And as that struggle to survive went on for hundreds of thousands of years, so our anxiety levels were always quite heightened.

But as I said, anxiety is created through negative thoughts - it's not the events themselves that create anxiety, but the thoughts we surround those events with. Life is simply a list of events. Our day-to-day life is a series of events that occur from one moment to the next, and it's how we think about those events and how we respond to those events that determines whether we're relaxed and calm or whether we're anxious and worried.

What's Been Good About Your Day?

Write down a list of 3 things that have been GOOD about your day, no matter how small or insignificant you might think them to be. Feel free to write more if you want to.

1. _____

   _____

2. _____

   _____

3. _____

   _____

Now listen to the MP3.

Case History: Carl

Karen called me on Saturday. It was about her boyfriend Carl. He was drinking heavily. In fact he was on a bender as we spoke, locked in his room in his flat with cases of beer getting hammered. He'd been like this for the last week. He'd called off work sick, but she knew they knew. If he didn't sort it out by Tuesday he would lose the lot: his flat, his job, his relationship.

I gave Karen the phone numbers for the rehab unit she asked about and I said I'd be happy to have a chat with Carl if he wanted to, but he would have to call me.

The next day, Sunday, I received an email from Carl. He would like to have a talk but he needed to dry out. He needed to see his doctor to get signed off work and he would call me.

Carl arranged for an initial consultation the following Saturday. He told me about the family issues that had triggered his drinking. How his father had died recently. All the details, all the reasons it was all too much. I listened.

Then we had a talk about how the brain works, how depression, anxiety and anger are created, why we suffer the way we do, and what we could do about our suffering.

As I talked, Carl became more and more engaged. It was wonderful to watch the pennies drop and to see him shift from trying to work out all the reasons and causes for his drinking, who did what to who, and begin to see how his anxiety, those loops of negativity were triggering behaviour patterns in the primitive brain. He saw his stress bucket full of worry and anxiety, all the negativity he had surrounded the events of his life with.

Carl and I saw each other 15 times. On our fifth session Carl didn't show up. I sent him an email to see if all was okay. He called me a few days later. He was very apologetic, full of remorse.

'Is everything okay?' I asked.

'I didn't think you'd want to see me,' he said.

'Why is that?'

'I had a drink.'

'Okay,' I said, 'do you want to talk about it?'

'Well, I had an argument with Karen and I went down to the bottle shop, bought a dozen cans of beer and I sat down to drink them. I'd just finished the second can and I sat there and I thought what the hell am I doing?'

'Then what happened?'

'Well, that stuff we've been talking about started coming into my head. That intellectual brain stuff, you know, proper assessment and all that. Well I sat there with an empty can in my hand, 10 more to go, and I just thought 'Sod this' and I poured the rest down the sink. I was kind of all over the place for the rest of the weekend. I didn't come to our session 'cos I thought I'd failed, I'd let everyone down again I suppose.'

'Well done,' I said

'Why's that? I had a bloody drink again.'

'Yes, and then you took control. That part of your brain that wants you to be the best Carl you can be took over and said 'enough'. That's brilliant, well done.'

I explained I wasn't here to judge Carl and he wasn't doing this to prove anything to me. The more conscious and aware he was of his thoughts, his emotions and his behaviour, the more he could trust himself to deal with the events and situations in his life in a calm, confident, self-assured manner.

The last time I spoke with Carl he was getting to the gym four times a week and he had been promoted in his job. His relationship had its rocky patches but he was dealing with it all without alcohol.

What's Been Good About Your Day?

Write down a list of 3 things that have been GOOD about your day, no matter how small or insignificant you might think them to be. Feel free to write more if you want to.

1. _____

   _____

2. _____

   _____

3. _____

   _____

Now listen to the MP3.

Listening To The MP3

You can't do the MP3 wrong. All you have to do is put your headphones on and press PLAY and you've done it right. It doesn't matter if you fall asleep.

What we're doing with the MP3 is creating a relaxed state of mind, bringing on the REM pattern that allows us to empty the stress bucket in a very calm, relaxed place. And we're also utilising the power of trance to bring the subconscious mind and the conscious mind into balance. So they begin co-operating and communicating, working together, balanced and focused, taking on board the positive suggestions and influences in that state of heightened relaxation that allows you to really move effortlessly into having control over your thoughts and your feelings, emptying that stress bucket, starting the day feeling very calm and relaxed and energised.

Thoughts will come and thoughts will go – that's what mind does, it *thinks*. So just allow the mind to wander. Every time you listen to the MP3 it will be different. Thoughts come and go like clouds drifting across the sky – they appear, they're there, and then they disappear. That's what thoughts are. But all the time the sky remains, just like the mind, and your subconscious mind will be picking up all the positive suggestions and influences.

So if you fall asleep that's okay, if you're awake all the way through, that's okay. You can't do it wrong.

What's Been Good About Your Day?

Write down a list of 3 things that have been GOOD about your day, no matter how small or insignificant you might think them to be. Feel free to write more if you want to.

1. _____

   _____

2. _____

   _____

3. _____

   _____

Now listen to the MP3.

Case History: Jennifer

Jennifer is a concert violinist. She suffered chronic performance anxiety. When we met she was anxious just talking about it. She felt hot and clammy and short of breath, and was emotional throughout the initial consultation.

Jennifer explained how her total lack of confidence meant she always loitered on the edge of the group, taking the furthest seat in the orchestra. The dialogue in her head was that she was no good and if she kept really quiet nobody would even notice her.

I asked her how long she had been working as a violinist. She said she had been working with local orchestras and quartets for about six years since leaving college. I asked Jennifer if she had worked in other musical environments besides classical concerts.

'Oh yes,' she replied, and named some well-known artists she had recorded with. 'But just in the string section,' she said.

'So you have regular work in various groups and situations and that's how you make your living?' I asked.

'Yes.'

'So why do you think you keep getting booked as violinist for these projects?'

Jennifer began to cry. 'I don't know, obviously they can't get anyone else so they must just end up calling me. I practice and practice and the more I practice the more I hear how bad I am, all the little mistakes, all the parts I could play so much better.'

At our first session I asked Jennifer the Miracle Question: 'If you wake up tomorrow and a Miracle had occurred while you were asleep, what small thing would be different about your week ahead?'

'I'd be enjoying my violin practice,' she said.

'What would you be practising?'

'There's this lovely Mozart piece I've been wanting to learn, so I'd start on that.'

'And how would you know you felt more confident with your practice?'

'I'd just enjoy playing the piece, and I wouldn't care how long I practiced for. If I wanted to play for half an hour that would be okay, and if I wanted to play for 2 hours that would be okay.'

In our fourth session I asked Jennifer what had been good about her week. She told me she'd been booked for a recording session the previous week, and the strangest thing was she actually felt excited about it. There were still some nerves when she arrived at the studio but she found herself laughing and joking with the other musicians. She noticed she was very relaxed and came away from the recording session with some great new contacts and lots of positive feedback. The thing that really amazed her was how natural it felt, interacting in a light way.

When I asked her the Miracle Question (what would let her know a miracle had occurred while she was asleep), she quickly replied:

'I'd be lighter about everything.'

'How would you know you had lightened up?'

'I'd be laughing more and I wouldn't care so much. I'd be happy to be working and realising I don't have to be the greatest soloist in the world,' she said.

Over the next few weeks Jennifer continued to make wonderful progress, feeling happier and more confident. I met her at the door for our eighth session and she had a big smile on her face and a sparkle in her eye.

'You're going to ask me what's been good about my week, aren't you?'

'Yes,' I replied, intrigued.

'Good,' she said, 'because the most amazing thing happened. I've been rehearsing with this orchestra and last week I was sitting out the back and the first violinist was so stressed, she was nearly in tears. She's quite good but she has this solo section in one of the big pieces and she's in a total state over it. She's so worried she's thinking about quitting. So anyway, while she's telling me all this I just said: 'I know that solo, I'll do it if you want'. She stopped and just looked at me and said, 'Really, would you?' I said 'Yeah sure', so we went and spoke to the conductor and he was fine with that – he just wants the piece played well.'

Jennifer laughed, 'So now I'm sitting in the first violin's chair, taking the solo, in a concert orchestra, under the nose of the conductor. And the weird thing is I don't care, I really don't care. It's like as soon as I stopped trying to be the great soloist and started to be light about my music, my life, it all got so much easier. It's really amazing.'

What's Been Good About Your Day?

Write down a list of 3 things that have been GOOD about your day, no matter how small or insignificant you might think them to be. Feel free to write more if you want to.

1. _____

_____

2. _____

_____

3. _____

_____

Now listen to the MP3.

How To Practice Being In Your Intellectual Mind

The intellectual mind is something we don't share with other animals. They don't use computers, they don't drive cars, they don't build mobile phones. Our intellectual mind allows us to dream and imagine the future. It allows us to innovate new ideas, invent ways to build new objects, to expand new thoughts and concepts. It's the creative part of our mind.

It's also that part of the mind where time and space seem to disappear - where you're painting a picture, or enjoying a view, or writing a letter, and you realise you've been doing this for an hour when you planned to do it for 10 minutes, and time has just slipped away. You're so engrossed in the creative process, whatever it is.

This intellectual part of your brain, the Left Prefrontal Cortex, is the part that you know as 'you' - the conscious part of your mind. So simply by becoming conscious of your thoughts, you've moved into the intellectual part of your mind. That's where we can make a proper assessment of a situation and come up with solutions. When we're seeing things clearly and coming up with innovative ways to solve problems or create new opportunities, then we are in control. We feel calm and relaxed.

You'll notice that when you get into that anxious, worried state - overwhelmed by a constant stream of negative thoughts - you're not even aware that you're doing it. And it can go on and on and on, and then you snap out of it at some point and think 'How long have I spent doing that?'

As soon as we get conscious of our thoughts, we've moved into the intellectual part of our mind. As soon as we get conscious that we're having negative thoughts, we're already in that Left Prefrontal Cortex because we have the *awareness*, and that's the trick. We don't need to take it any further, we don't need to make any judgement – we just need to become aware of the thought.

And when we get into the intellectual part of our brain, because it's the conscious part, the part that we know as us, it allows us to make a proper assessment of situations and come up with solutions. As we practise being aware of our thoughts, so we'll spend less time in that primitive part of our brain, and more time in the intellectual part of the brain where we have control.

What's Been Good About Your Day?

Write down a list of 3 things that have been GOOD about your day, no matter how small or insignificant you might think them to be. Feel free to write more if you want to.

1. _____

_____

2. _____

_____

3. _____

_____

Now listen to the MP3.

Case History: Janet

Janet came to see me – she had been referred by her doctor. She was signed off work with stress and anxiety.

Janet was finalising her divorce. Property was being contested and her ex-husband had made threats and was behaving in an intimidating, aggressive way.

Janet wasn't sleeping and nighttime was worse as the anxiety and fear increased. She was exhausted all the time with no motivation. Emails were piling up and the process of moving on was grinding to a halt as fear and anxiety took over.

I explained to Janet how the brain works. How we have that powerful, creative part of our brain, the Left Prefrontal Cortex, where we make a proper assessment of situations, come up with solutions and generally feel calm, happy and in control of our life. Then there is that other part, the primitive part, the fight or flight depression part of the brain.

'Yep, that's me alright,' she said.

When we operate from that part of the brain we feel anxious, depressed, angry and frustrated.

The pennies were starting to drop.

'Oh yeah that's me.'

This part of the brain is also very negative, so it's only going to see all the things that are wrong with the situation. It's going to want to run away and hide.

'Yep,' she interrupted, 'like those emails, I just want them to disappear. I can't open the mail because I've already made up my mind it's full of more problems.'

'It's also a very obsessive part of the brain,' I continued.

'Oh dear yes, I'm just sick of the sound of my own voice. The only thing I seem to talk to anyone about is this bloody divorce and...'

'It's also very vigilant, it's constantly scanning the horizon looking for possible threats, and it will even make up problems that will never...'

'Yes, yes, yes!' she almost screamed, 'I lie awake at night worrying about him breaking into the house, and doing the most awful things. Whenever I'm out I'm terrified about what might be happening back at the house. Oh my god.'

'And all this anxiety, all of this worry, is just negative thoughts,' I said. 'It's not the events in our life that cause anxiety. It's the negative thoughts we surround those events with that cause anxiety.'

Janet was silent. She looked at me out the corner of her eye for a moment. She thought about this some more.

'That's true,' she said quietly. 'Those emails are just things to be dealt with to resolve these problems. And if I really think about it, he is sad and angry. My anxiety is just his desperation to try and get control. Really I just need to get on with it and stop worrying about things that will never happen.'

'And as your sleep pattern comes back to normal, and you start emptying that stress bucket, you'll wake up energised and positive, motivated to get on with it,' I said. 'And through all of this your brain is going to help you. It will begin that wonderful process of creating serotonin, that powerful neurotransmitter that makes us calm, coping, brave individuals, positively active, interacting positively again with the world around us, and feeling and thinking positively again. You will be back in your intellectual mind, back in control of your thoughts, in control of your feelings and in control of your behaviour. Calm, relaxed and confident.'

What's Been Good About Your Day?

Write down a list of 3 things that have been GOOD about your day, no matter how small or insignificant you might think them to be. Feel free to write more if you want to.

1. _____

   _____

2. _____

   _____

3. _____

   _____

Now listen to the MP3.

Why We Ask 'What's Been Good About Your Day?'

Every day the question is: 'What's been good about your day?' This is a very powerful exercise. For you to recall a list of things that have been positive about your day, you have to go into the Left Prefrontal Cortex part of your brain to access that file of pleasant, positive memories. So we're constantly practising the act of going to and being in that Left Prefrontal Cortex.

The other thing that's very powerful about this exercise is that all through your day now you know that this is the question you will have to answer before you press PLAY on the MP3. So your subconscious mind is storing away all those positive events from the day knowing that you're compiling a really positive list for when that question has to be answered this evening, when you put pen to paper. It is constantly keeping your mind in the Left Prefrontal Cortex, the intellectual part of your brain, building up that string of neurons, creating those new pathways, positive pathways, that allow you to see and be in control of your thoughts, in control of your feelings, and in control of your behaviour.

The other thing that happens through considering the question 'What 's been good about your day?' is it creates the habit of gratitude. Gratitude is a very powerful, positive practice – that ability just to be quietly grateful for the good things that happen in our day. Because it's the little things that matter. We're all aware when something big or wonderful happens but it's that constant awareness of the small things, the positive events that make up our day, recognising them and being grateful for them.

And as we do that, we're literally spending more time in the Left Prefrontal Cortex of our brain, that intellectual part of our mind, that part of us which makes a proper assessment of our life and lets us feel grateful and happy about the positive things that have happened during our day. And by acknowledging these good things, we become conscious, creating those habits of calmness, confidence and happiness.

What's Been Good About Your Day?

Write down a list of 3 things that have been GOOD about your day, no matter how small or insignificant you might think them to be. Feel free to write more if you want to.

1. _____

   _____

2. _____

   _____

3. _____

   _____

Now listen to the MP3.

Case History: Mike

Mike was moving to Spain. He had finally made the big decision he had been toying with for years. He'd finalised the rent on his flat, sold most of his possessions and put the rest in storage. His bags were packed and in ten days' time he would touch down in Barcelona to begin his new life.

Mike was terrified when he called me.

'What have I done?' he exclaimed on the phone. 'What was I thinking? I can't do this – I don't know anyone, I don't have a job when I get there, I haven't even heard from the person I'm supposed to be staying with for over a week. What if they've changed their mind? Oh no, what have I done!'

I saw Mike later that day. He was still very anxious. He hadn't been sleeping well for weeks and it was getting worse. He was waking up at 2am with raging panic attacks.

Mike is a qualified English language teacher. He was tired of the routine life he had been living and had always dreamed of using his skills to travel and live in exotic places.

At the initial consultation we talked about how the brain works. Mike recognised immediately that his intellectual brain had made an assessment of his life and come up with some options and solutions. He had acted on these ideas and everything had flowed effortlessly towards realising that goal. He had sorted out his flat, sold things he didn't need, put a safety net of money in the bank, and he'd organised somewhere to stay for the first month in Spain until he got orientated. He had even applied for some jobs in Barcelona!

But as his departure date drew nearer he had begun to lose intellectual control and his primitive, emotional mind started to take over. He began to lose the excited, confident feelings and began to feel anxious. He started to feel negative – what if he couldn't get a job? What would he do if the people he'd arranged to stay with changed their mind? People change their mind all the time and he didn't know them very well – they might not answer the phone, or return his emails. He couldn't just turn up without some more communication. Oh and he couldn't stay here – he'd cancelled his rental agreement, he'd given up that lovely flat he was starting to miss (and is this such a bad a place to live after all?) and he'd sold his television and his bed! More negativity, more obsessive thoughts about all the things that might go wrong. Mike was starting to create scenarios in his head that would never happen… but might.

The penny was beginning to drop for Mike as he started to see how his thoughts were creating his anxiety. All anxiety is created through negative thoughts. It's not the events in our life that cause anxiety, it's the thoughts we surround those events with.

Mike began to realise that he had done a brilliant job of preparing himself for this move, that everything was in its place and that with a few more phone calls and an email or two, events would continue to unfold in the way he had planned. Mike saw very clearly that by shifting his thoughts he could very quickly get back in control of his life.

I saw Mike for two more sessions over the next week. During that week Mike listened to the MP3 – the same MP3 that comes with this book. We did two Solution Focused Hypnotherapy sessions. At our last session, when I asked Mike what had been good about his week, he said he had spoken to the people he would be staying with and they were excited about his arrival. He had sent off some more job applications and he had received a positive reply to another

application. Two weeks later I received an email from Mike –
it said 'Thank you!'

What's Been Good About Your Day?

Write down a list of 3 things that have been GOOD about your day, no matter how small or insignificant you might think them to be. Feel free to write more if you want to.

1. _____

_____

2. _____

_____

3. _____

_____

Now listen to the MP3.

A Bit About Mindfulness (Attentiveness)

Mindfulness is all about *attention* and *awareness*. It is about getting to know who we really are. Mindfulness is the 'Acceptance of Being'. I call it 'Attentiveness'.

We all spend so much time in our heads *doing*. Then we project these things we 'should be doing' out into our lives, and we feel responsible or overwhelmed, sometimes bored, guilty, unworthy and exhausted. Focusing on the global goal, the result that seems so far away, striving and getting more anxious and overwhelmed as we gauge our achievements.

We perceive our thoughts and the feelings we attach to those thoughts as how things really are. Never questioning the thought, or the source of the thought or feeling. It is the reality we accept.

Mindfulness is the practice of seeing our thoughts. It is the simple act of Being instead of Doing.

It begins with acceptance. Accepting that it is okay to just *be* for a moment. Allowing a time to check in with what is happening in our mind. And a curiosity to just sit and observe. Not judging. Not trying.

Just as the body breathes without conscious thought, without constantly checking that we are doing it right, we begin the *practice* of Mindfulness by passively observing our breathing. Focusing on the simple sensation of air passing in through the tip of our nose, and out through the tip of our nose... in through the tip of our nose, and out through the tip of our nose. Using the conscious awareness of breathing as an anchor for our thoughts.

The daily practice of Mindfulness is a powerful therapeutic resource in its own right. The Mindfulness technique practiced in the current modern Western style is a structured, secular approach to mind-training skills taught and practiced in Eastern Philosophies and Religions. Mindfulness is a direct descendent of the 'calm-abiding' meditation practiced in Buddhism for over two thousand years. It promotes calmness and happiness, well-being and deep-centred peace, as well as clarity and awareness.

Now, having been put under the modern microscope of clinical testing and scientific analysis, this meditation technique has been proven to greatly help with pain management, anger management, relationships, clinical depression, anxiety, confidence, weight management, insomnia and performance enhancement.

Mindfulness is a practice. It is a regular exercise that is the end in itself. It pays back very quickly in so many ways: lowering blood pressure, increasing attention and appreciation of the good things in life, lowering anxiety and lifting depression. And through the conscious engagement with reality, being in the present moment, we are more aware of our conscious choices.

Not living our life on autopilot, we can appreciate the sensations and joys of the experience of living rather than analysing everything. We can suspend our expectations, our fantasies about how it should have been, or could be, accepting who we are and letting go of the energy-sapping striving for a while.

Through Mindfulness we start to recognise the vast array of thoughts floating across the backdrop of our minds, seeing them for what they are – just thoughts, mental events, not real, only imagined.

And as we consciously acknowledge and approach our thoughts we begin to see the illusory nature of the thoughts we react to as real. How, just like a mist, there is nothing to be avoided. That by approaching and observing, we can see clearly how they are just thoughts. All the time keeping us consciously in the present moment, not travelling in time to the past or the future.

As we carry the calm-abiding stillness into our reality after each session, we can really appreciate the energising, nurturing, nourishing effect the practice of Mindfulness has on our day-to-day life.

What's Been Good About Your Day?

Write down a list of 3 things that have been GOOD about your day, no matter how small or insignificant you might think them to be. Feel free to write more if you want to.

1. _____

   _____

2. _____

   _____

3. _____

   _____

Now listen to the MP3.

Case History: James

James loved his horse. Riding was his passion and, outside work, he spent most of his time with his horse Aladdin.

Three months before we met, Aladdin had thrown James in a moment of fright while out on a ride. A car had driven past quite fast and startled Aladdin, who had reared up and James came off. He was battered and bruised but not badly hurt. Over the next few months James was struggling with his fear of getting back in the saddle. The delicate relationship he had with Aladdin felt strained and James felt more and more anxious the longer he put off riding, while at the same time feeling guilty and frustrated about his communication with Aladdin.

Over the five sessions we had together, James became very conscious of negative thoughts with which he had surrounded the event of riding. How his primitive mind was constantly vigilant and on guard, looking for future threats and reminding him of how bad that fall could have been.

As his intellectual mind took back control of his life, as James became conscious of what he was thinking, getting in control of his feelings and emotions, back in control of his actions, he began helping Aladdin to do the same. Gently walking him out in the yard. Getting him used to the saddle again. Communicating and interacting positively with Aladdin.

He started gently riding him through his exercises around the field and over the period of a few weeks they supported each other as they actively focused on building that trust up again and enjoying their long weekend rides in the hills, the bond between them stronger than ever for the conscious effort they had made.

What's Been Good About Your Day?

Write down a list of 3 things that have been GOOD about your day, no matter how small or insignificant you might think them to be. Feel free to write more if you want to.

1. _____

_____

2. _____

_____

3. _____

_____

Now listen to the MP3.

What Is REM And The Stress Bucket?

REM, Rapid Eye Movement, is a part of our sleep pattern. When we go to bed at night we have that first period where we may have just finished reading and we're dozing off, and from there we slip into REM sleep.

REM sleep lasts for a specific period of time; it's about 20% of our sleep pattern. From REM sleep we go into deep sleep which rejuvenates the physical body. But the REM period is very important – that's the part of our sleep where we start emptying the stress bucket. REM sleep is where we deal with the unresolved emotional issues from the previous day.

So during REM, either through metaphorical or clear dreaming, we'll take those unresolved emotional situations of the day and we'll move them from the primitive part of our brain into the intellectual part of our brain where we have control over them. That's why often we wake up in the morning and that thing that was really annoying us the day before just doesn't annoy us any more – in fact, we've probably forgotten about it.

What's Been Good About Your Day?

Write down a list of 3 things that have been GOOD about your day, no matter how small or insignificant you might think them to be. Feel free to write more if you want to.

1. _____

_____

2. _____

_____

3. _____

_____

Now listen to the MP3.

Case History: Claire

Claire was feeling lost, stuck. In her early 40s and highly educated, Claire had a degree in environmental science and enjoyed music and art. She hadn't done any of the above for a while now. When we met Claire was packing shelves in a supermarket four nights a week and spent her time wondering what had happened to her life. The more she thought about all the lost time, what she hadn't achieved, the more 'stuck' she felt.

At our initial consultation, after Claire had told me how she was feeling – her depression about where she found herself now and her anxiety about what to do next – I asked her the question I ask everyone quite early on in our sessions.

'If someone waved a magic wand and life was how you wanted it to be right now, what would be happening, what would you be doing?'

'I guess I'd be studying again. I would really like to do a Masters in some kind of environmental studies… it's just that I feel…'

'That's a wonderful idea,' I interrupted.

'Yes, I really enjoyed my time at university,' she went on. She laughed to herself, 'I actually had a social life there too.'

'What did you enjoy doing in your spare time?'

'Now? Nothing. I hardly go…'

'No, when you were at university.'

'Oh I joined lots of groups. There was always some event to participate in, or watch, or organise. It's funny, I'm remembering this night we put on a Green Rave and somebody organised a PA system for all the bands and DJs where all the electricity was run by pedal power. We had a bank of exercise bikes along the back of the tent and people had to keep pedalling or the lights went dim and the music cut out... I wonder where that thought came from...'

Claire and I saw each other five times. On our third session, in her list of what had been good about her week, she had joined a local theatre group and was helping to source and make the costumes for their next production. She had also gone out to see some live music. And Claire had been on the internet exploring the possibilities for further study.

On our fifth session, Claire bounced into the room. I didn't even get the 'What's been good...' question out of my mouth before she burst out with: 'I did it! I've found the course I'm going to do. I spoke to the university on the phone and they were very encouraging. They said my qualifications fit perfectly with the course and to get my application in. So I did. And it's the strangest thing - that shelf-packing job that has been such a curse for so long? It's perfect! It means I have the right hours and an income while I get back into a study routine...'

Claire sent me an email a few weeks later to let me know she had received her place on her MA course.

What's Been Good About Your Day?

Write down a list of 3 things that have been GOOD about your day, no matter how small or insignificant you might think them to be. Feel free to write more if you want to.

1. _____

   _____

2. _____

   _____

3. _____

   _____

Now listen to the MP3.

Why Do We Listen To The MP3?

The MP3 helps us on many different levels. It relaxes and calms us, and when we're calm and relaxed it helps the serotonin start to flow. It also brings on the state of REM so it helps us to empty that stress bucket. It helps very much with our sleep patterns. As we get more and more relaxed and calm in the mind, we sleep through the night, and as we sleep a lot better we wake up feeling refreshed and energised and positive in the morning.

There are also some very positive influences and suggestions in the MP3. It takes you into that wonderful balanced state of trance where the subconscious mind and conscious mind are working together, focused and taking on board those positive influences and suggestions to help on a subconscious level. We start to really feel more energised and we begin changing the way our mind works – as we change our thoughts it allows us to change our feelings and our behaviour.

We listen to the MP3 every night because habits are created through repetition and that habit of calming the mind, of sleeping well, of emptying the stress bucket, of hearing the same thing over and over, creates those wonderful new neural pathways in our minds.

It's a bit like going to the gym every day and lifting weights. If you want a toned, healthy body, you don't go to the gym twice a month and lift small weights. You go to the gym regularly, going through the routine, increasing the weights, and over a very short period of time – in a matter of days even – you start to feel more toned. In a matter of weeks, you're feeling stronger and seeing your body change – the muscles are getting bigger and the definition is increasing. This also feeds the motivation to do more of the same – to go to the gym and practice more and lift bigger weights, to keep taking each positive step, building up the momentum.

Just as we can do that with the physical body, we can do it with the mind. Listening to the MP3 every night builds up the momentum, keeps the momentum going, increasing the neurological changes in our brain which end up expressing themselves through positive change in our day-to-day life.

What's Been Good About Your Day?

Write down a list of 3 things that have been GOOD about your day, no matter how small or insignificant you might think them to be. Feel free to write more if you want to.

1. _____

   _____

2. _____

   _____

3. _____

   _____

Now listen to the MP3.

Case History: Stacey

Stacey was really suffering. She was in tears within minutes of sitting down. Anxiety ruled her life. It held her down in every area of her life: constant feelings of incompetence, inferiority, fear of authority figures - and everyone seemed to be an authority figure.

Her relationship with her husband was falling apart and every day felt like it would be her last day at work. Stacey was constantly worried that her colleagues or her boss would realise how incompetent she was at her job and she would be sacked. Her career in the legal world meant her day was a string of meetings with police and lawyers and she spent most of the day feeling physically ill, sweating and blushing. It was driving her and those close to her crazy.

I asked Stacey how long she had been in this job.

'Seven years,' she replied.

Over the next eleven weeks of sessions Stacey showed wonderful progress. At our first session I asked her where she thought her confidence was on a scale of 1 to 10. She said she was probably 3/10.

I asked her to imagine for a moment that as she slept peacefully tonight, a magic wand was waved and when she woke tomorrow a miracle had occurred and she realised she was feeling 4/10 confident – a subtle change had occurred.

'What small changes would you notice during the next few days that let you know a miracle had occurred?'

'I'd have a conversation with someone at work and feel relaxed,' she answered. 'And I'd get to work and the first thing I'd do is open some emails… I know that sounds really stupid but I just put them off and put them off,' she added.

132

'Great,' I replied. 'Tonight, while you sleep, that magic wand gets waved and you know things have changed, that your confidence has gone up to 4/10, and this week you get to work and the first thing you do is start opening and checking emails. And you really know that magic wand is doing its stuff when you realise you're having a conversation with a colleague and you just feel calm and relaxed. Fantastic!'

Over the next few weeks Stacey began to notice changes. Her list of 'What's been good about your week?' was growing. At our fifth session it included: 'Work is going well. I attended a meeting and handled it really well, even offered an opinion.' Stacey scaled her confidence at 6/10.

It was our seventh session when Stacey came bounding into the room. She hadn't even sat down and she was already giving me her list of good things.

'I've been to lots of meetings this week and I've spoken up about a few things. I really feel like I've contributed and the strange thing is people have agreed with me – and they've listened, they've actually listened to me. That's not all though. My boss has asked me to make a presentation to the whole department about this new system that we're introducing. And it's like I'm a little bit nervous, and this is going to sound really weird, but I know I can do it.'

'That doesn't sound weird to...'

'AND – I've been asked out on a girls' night out after work on Friday. I don't drink and I never really get asked and I don't know what I'll do or what I'll wear – but I said yes. Wow!'

'Where is your confidence at then?' I got in quick with a big smile.

'Oh at least 8/10, at least.'

Over the next few weeks Stacey continued seeing the changes. At our last session she scaled herself at 9/10 – she was taking on more responsibility, she had delivered her presentation and had really enjoyed it. She received a glowing assessment from her boss and she was now actively looking for opportunities for promotion in her organisation. Her relationship with her husband was much better and her social life had improved immensely as she realised how good it was to go out with people and just enjoy herself.

At the end of our last session I asked Stacey what changes she was aware of over the last few months.

'One big thing is I don't constantly check things anymore. I don't need to check emails five times – I write them and press send. I get so much more done. And I'm not asking people questions all the time – I use my initiative much more. In fact I notice other people who are always asking questions and not just getting on with it. I notice people look at me and talk to me in a different way, like they accept or respect me. But you know the big thing I've noticed? I realise how many other people are suffering just like I was. How they talk and how they act like I used to behave only a few months ago.'

What's Been Good About Your Day?

Write down a list of 3 things that have been GOOD about your day, no matter how small or insignificant you might think them to be. Feel free to write more if you want to.

1. _____

   _____

2. _____

   _____

3. _____

   _____

Now listen to the MP3.

Serotonin And Why We Need It

Serotonin makes us feel brave and confident, which helps us deal with any situation. Serotonin is a neurotransmitter that is created in the brain and acts as a catalyst for positive mental behaviour. So as serotonin begins to flow we feel calm and relaxed, we feel motivated, we feel confident.

Even in situations that may be a bit challenging where we need to feel confident, it's that brave chemical serotonin that allows us to deal with situations as they arise. When we're in balance, when our thoughts are in balance, we create a constant steady flow of serotonin that allows us to deal with situations in a calm, relaxed, self-assured way.

When we're suffering from depression, we're not making any serotonin – it's just stopped. And that's why when you're depressed, the doctor will prescribe anti-depressants to try and get that serotonin flowing again in a nice, steady flow.

When we're feeling anxious and worried, we're creating a mass of neurotransmitters like adrenaline, noradrenaline and cortisol, often at all the wrong times so our sleep pattern is disrupted, and we're not making any serotonin.

It's when we're operating within the intellectual part of our brain, making a proper assessment of situations, coming up with solutions, and getting on with our life, that we start that drip feed of serotonin. Allowing us to feel calm and relaxed, confident and self-assured.

What's Been Good About Your Day?

Write down a list of 3 things that have been GOOD about your day, no matter how small or insignificant you might think them to be. Feel free to write more if you want to.

1. _____

_____

2. _____

_____

3. _____

_____

Now listen to the MP3.

Case History: Lisa

Lisa is 30, professional, attractive and wanting a relationship. She is confident in most situations but when it comes to men she falls apart inside. Her calm, relaxed self runs away and in her words, she turns into an anxious, confused, needy little girl. Her relationships have been short and fraught, or distant, aloof and non-committal. Lisa has tried various therapies but she keeps arriving back at the same place.

We started with an explanation of how the brain works, why we suffer from anxiety and what we can do about it.

Lisa engaged immediately in the conversation. I explained how the Left Prefrontal Cortex, the intellectual part of the brain, generally gets things right – it makes a proper assessment of a situation and comes up with answers and solutions.

'That's where I am all day at work,' she said. 'I love my work. In fact it's the best part of my life. I guess I feel in control at work. It's the rest of the time...'

'Exactly,' I said. 'There is another part, the primitive, emotional part of the brain. It's also known as the 'fight or flight' part of the brain.'

'Oh my God,' she said, 'that's me, that's me! That is me in a sentence when it comes to relationships. When I meet someone, even before I've finished the first drink, I'm either behaving all prickly and edgy or I just want to run away.'

I smiled and went on. I explained the different ways that our primitive brain operates and presents itself in our thoughts and actions. This primitive, emotional part of the brain always defaults to the parameters of depression, anxiety and anger, or a combination of these. It's also a very negative part of the brain.

'Oh that's me all right. I get sick of hearing myself constantly banging on about how lonely I am, and how so and so is just a loser. Honestly sometimes it's just embarrassing the way I carry on about it with my girlfriends.'

'That's right...'

'And I get so angry about it. Mainly with myself, but sometimes it just seems to spill over to...' She put her head in her hands and shook herself. 'Aarrgh!'

'This is good,' I said. 'You are getting conscious about these thoughts and behaviours.'

I went on explaining how it was also a very obsessive part of the brain.

Lisa sat there looking at the page in front of her as I wrote this down, alternately nodding and shaking her head.

'Yep,' she said.

'It's also a very vigilant part of the brain,' I said. 'Hypervigilant, constantly scanning your world looking for more perceived threats, and reasons why everything will go wrong.'

'That's me and men. I've met them, married them, fought with them, they've cheated on me and we're divorced, all before they've even told me their name,' she said.

'And you can see how all these feelings and emotions, all this anxiety is created from negative thoughts. It's not the event of meeting a man and having a drink and a conversation that causes anxiety – it's the thoughts we surround these events with that cause anxiety.'

Lisa looked at me – the fog was clearing as she grasped this concept.

Over the following days and weeks and months, Lisa became conscious of the good things in her day. She started seeing the small changes, those miracles occurring in her week, every night listening to the MP3 and becoming calmer, more relaxed and taking control of her thoughts, her feelings and her behaviour.

What's Been Good About Your Day?

Write down a list of 3 things that have been GOOD about your day, no matter how small or insignificant you might think them to be. Feel free to write more if you want to.

1. _____

   _____

2. _____

   _____

3. _____

   _____

Now listen to the MP3.

How Do We Get Serotonin Flowing?

The flow of Serotonin is created through positive activity and positive action. That doesn't have to be major physical activity or exercise – it could be simply going for a walk. It could be just tidying up around the house when we haven't done that for a while, sorting that pile of papers in the corner, clearing a desk that's got overwhelmingly cluttered. It could be making a nice meal, it could be going for a walk in the garden.

Serotonin is also generated through positive interaction so perhaps picking up the phone, just saying hello to an old friend, or taking that invitation for a cup of tea can be a very good start to get serotonin flowing. Changes begin small and then they grow bigger and bigger so making those early changes is the key. It's not the big stuff, it's doing the little stuff, and getting the serotonin flowing in a nice, even, regular way.

Positive thinking is a big factor in starting the flow of serotonin in our brain. Doing the MP3 every night is a positive thought process put into action. Having the thought 'I'm going to do this' is the positive thought. Pressing PLAY is the positive action. It will allow you to feel calm and relaxed and it will motivate you further. Just like the positive thought: 'Yes I will go and have a cup of tea with my friend.'

Serotonin is stimulated through a combination of these conditions. The positive thought of going for a walk leads to physical movement and a stroll in the park or by the river. This leads to fresh air and some positive interaction with nature and the world outside. Perhaps at some point this positive action will lead to positive interaction with another person (or your favourite dog), sharing the walk along the river with a friend.

And as we start doing those small things, they grow and grow and we start seeing all those little positive moments – positive actions, positive interactions, and positive thoughts – joining together as small events during each day and becoming more and more grateful for them. Then of course we're already in that intellectual part of our brain and the serotonin is flowing and we're becoming calm, relaxed, and self-assured.

What's Been Good About Your Day?

Write down a list of 3 things that have been GOOD about your day, no matter how small or insignificant you might think them to be. Feel free to write more if you want to.

1. _____

_____

2. _____

_____

3. _____

_____

Now listen to the MP3.

Case History: Julian

Julian couldn't sleep. He woke wide-awake every night at 2:33am. Julian didn't have to look at the clock anymore. He knew what time it was, lying there in the dark, his wife fast asleep beside him. Most nights he got up and wandered the house for an hour or so. He made a hot drink, ate food, watched TV for a while. Finally he'd crawl back into bed and wrestle with sleep for a few hours until it was time to get up. Most mornings he watched the clock tick over and the alarm go off. Julian began every day stressed and tired.

He wasn't sure when it began but it had been going on for most of the year. He was irritable at work. Julian was a builder – he had a small crew of men and his company was always busy on a construction job somewhere. He had noticed that now he found it difficult dealing with clients. He hated answering the phone and spent a lot more time in his office 'hiding away', as he put it, so he didn't have to talk to people.

At the initial consultation we talked about the negative, anxious, primitive brain and how all that anxiety was caused by negative thoughts.

The penny really dropped when I explained how REM sleep empties the stress bucket. All our negative thoughts and anxieties are stashed away in this stress bucket but our mind and body have a wonderful process for emptying it. It is called Rapid Eye Movement or REM sleep. It is the process the mind uses to deal with the emotional events of the past few days. As we go into REM sleep we move the unresolved emotional events of the day from our primitive brain to our intellectual brain where we have control over them. Through either clear or metaphorical dreams that we don't even have to remember, we take control of past events. Often we wake up the next day and we've forgotten all about that thing that had us all worked up just the day before.

I explained to Julian that because REM lasted for about twenty percent of our sleep time, and we didn't get any overtime from it, when REM was over and we still had a stress bucket three quarters full we woke up very alert and often agitated, unable to sleep properly again. We use a lot of energy trying in vain to empty the stress bucket after REM has finished, and we finally wake exhausted and anxious. Before our feet have even hit the floor in the morning, we are pouring the negativity and stress back into the bucket, starting our day tired, anxious and negative.

I gave Julian the MP3 – the same MP3 that comes with this book. I explained to him how the MP3 begins to get that stress bucket emptied. How all he had to do, last thing at night, was press PLAY as he went off to sleep and allow the MP3 to do its work.

Soon he noticed he was sleeping better, occasionally waking in the night but not for long, and not getting up. It was not long before Julian was sleeping right through until his alarm woke him. He noticed he was more energised in the morning. He had more energy for his family and enjoyed morning time with his young sons over breakfast. He became more focused on the job, dealing with clients in a more positive way. A few of the men in his crew even commented that it was good to have him back.

What's Been Good About Your Day?

Write down a list of 3 things that have been GOOD about your day, no matter how small or insignificant you might think them to be. Feel free to write more if you want to.

1. _____

_____

2. _____

_____

3. _____

_____

Now listen to the MP3.

A Bit About Motivation

The more time we spend in our intellectual brain, living our life from that Left Prefrontal Cortex, the more confident and determined we are to achieve our goals. They don't have to be big goals, but they're goals – maybe we want to get fit, maybe get healthy, maybe stop smoking, maybe get that new job, maybe go out on a date, maybe increase our circle of friendships.

As we spend that time focused and calm and confident, our motivation grows. That determination and that motivation, powered by the constant steady flow of serotonin, allows us to calmly persist towards our goals. The wonderful thing about being motivated is what was once a struggle can become quite effortless. The more motivated we are, the more focused we are, the more committed we are, the easier life seems to flow.

The habit of positivity is created through repetition. So the more we practice it, the more motivated and energised we become, the more energy we've got, the more focused we become, and the more time we spend in our Left Prefrontal Cortex coming up with proper assessments of situations, coming up with wonderful new creative solutions.

And all that time we're emptying the stress bucket and creating more spare capacity inside our own head, literally space in our minds, which helps us come up with more innovative ideas on how to achieve those wonderful goals and dreams which again just feed the motivation and make us want to keep going.

And so it becomes a lovely cycle of motivation and energy, of positivity, of new ideas, of increased space and a flow that goes round and round, all the time powered by that wonderful neurotransmitter serotonin. And all travelling down that broad, new, neural pathway in our brain that we've created by changing our habits of mind.

What's Been Good About Your Day?

Write down a list of 3 things that have been GOOD about your day, no matter how small or insignificant you might think them to be. Feel free to write more if you want to.

1. _____

   _____

2. _____

   _____

3. _____

   _____

Now listen to the MP3.

Case History: Ashley

Ashley was four weeks away from sitting her final exams. Anxiety played a big part in Ashley's life. When we first met she had passed her driving test but refused to drive, she had few friends, her self-esteem was low and anxiety limited her socially.

Ashley had come a long way in the six weeks since we had our initial consultation. She was driving to our sessions on her own, she had started socialising with a new group of friends. Ashley's parents were very happy with the changes she had made and the whole family was enjoying her positive approach to life.

Ashley had told me she was anxious about her final exams that were coming up. I suggested she could focus the techniques we had been using on settling her exam nerves and enhancing her performance at the exams. Ashley had told me when we first met that she had been predicted by her teachers to get one A and two B's in her A-Level (final high school) results. When I asked her what she thought she would get she answered two B's and a C. Now six weeks on she felt she might manage the A and two B's her teachers had suggested.

I asked Ashley to scale between 1 and 10 her confidence level about achieving an A and two B's. She said about 5/10.

I asked her to imagine the magic wand being waved while she was asleep and a miracle occurring – what would be different about the week ahead that let her know she was 6/10 confident with her exams?

'I'd be revising more, and I'd be doing it everyday.'

'Great,' I said. 'So you're revising every day, and how do you know your confidence is increasing?'

'Time is passing easily. It's like I'm so focused on the study I don't notice the time passing.'

'Fantastic,' I said.

At our next session we talked about the exam situation. How all anxiety is created through negative thoughts. I asked Ashley to imagine she was outside the exam room waiting to go in and to tell me what she saw.

'All the people in my class are outside, and there's a group of girls I kind of hang out with and they are all anxious – they're telling each other how they haven't done enough study and they're sure they won't know what's on the paper.'

'So they're all talking over the top of each other and quite agitated.'

'Yes,' she said.

'Okay, now I want you to imagine the sort of person who is functioning from their intellectual brain. What are they doing?'

'They're standing to one side, in their own space.'

'How do they look?'

'They look pretty cool actually, kind of calm and aloof.'

'Great, what is that person feeling about this exam?'

'They're feeling like they've done all the revision they can. That they're probably going to know most of the questions on the paper.'

'How are the agitated group feeling about this person?'

Ashley laughed. 'They're probably more anxious 'cos she looks so calm.'

'Great, so if we waved our magic wand, where would you be standing outside the exam room?'

'I'd be standing off on my own feeling calm and relaxed, a bit aloof.'

'Excellent, and if we waved our magic wand and you were calm and relaxed, what sort of grades would you be able to achieve?'

'Definitely a B, maybe an A,' she said.

Over the next couple of sessions we continued working on confidence, and every day Ashley's confidence grew stronger and stronger. Our last session was two days before Ashley's exams. She was already feeling that if the magic wand was waved she might actually manage a couple of A's and a B.

I suggested that today we go for it. If that magic wand was waved and that miracle occurred when she woke up, what would be different about her week?

'I'd be feeling 10/10 confident outside that exam room. I would be in my own space, calm and aloof. The other girls in my class would notice, and I'd be okay about that.'

'And what grades would you go for if that miracle occurred?' I asked.

'I'd get 3 A's,' she replied, without missing a beat.

I didn't see Ashley again. However, I did get an email at the end of that summer. Ashley said she had had the best summer holiday, she went travelling with friends, she'd met a boy and she was accepted in to her first choice of university – Ashley had achieved two A's and one A star! She just wanted to say 'thank you'.

What's Been Good About Your Day?

Write down a list of 3 things that have been GOOD about your day, no matter how small or insignificant you might think them to be. Feel free to write more if you want to.

1. _____

_____

2. _____

_____

3. _____

_____

Now listen to the MP3.

The Power of Positive Thought

Like attracts like, so positive thinking attracts more positive thinking. It becomes a self-perpetuating process where creative, positive thoughts lead to even greater positive thoughts, finding new ways to innovate and consciously carry out more positive actions.

Another very powerful thing about positive thought is that it will always trump negative thoughts. And as we become more and more positive, we will find that we attract positive people and positive situations where we can express our positivity.

Those little negative things that have niggled and worried us tend to fall away and we find that we attract more and more positivity and more and more positive situations into our world. Just as your thoughts creates the feelings which creates your behaviour and your world, so positive thoughts will create positive feelings which will create positive actions and positive situations in your life.

So we've actually created a whole new way of thinking, feeling and behaving, each one attracting more of the same to itself, like a magnet. Then positive change becomes inevitable.

What's Been Good About Your Day?

Write down a list of 3 things that have been GOOD about your day, no matter how small or insignificant you might think them to be. Feel free to write more if you want to.

1. _____

   _____

2. _____

   _____

3. _____

   _____

Now listen to the MP3.

Performance Enhancement

Hypnotherapy is an incredibly powerful tool for improving performance in sport. The dramatic improvements achieved by elite athletes through the use of hypnosis are well-documented.

At the 1956 Olympics in Melbourne, Australia, the Russian Olympic team took eleven hypnotherapists to assist in the team's performance. Australian swimmers and British athletes use hypnosis to focus and improve their performance. Boxing is renowned for the use of hypnosis by champions. Glenn Catley, two-times World Super Middleweight Champion, makes no secret of the fact that hypnotherapy helped him become the best in the world. His hypnotherapist, David Newton, travelled the world with Glenn as an integral part of his pre-fight preparation team. David Newton was my teacher in Hypnotherapy and Psychotherapy.

But it is not just elite athletes who can benefit from hypnotherapy. I see many sportsmen and women, as well as musicians and actors, who want to improve their performance ability and their results in their chosen field. We may not all rise to the heights of international competition in our endeavours but hypnotherapy has been shown to greatly enhance our ability to improve performance results, and the level of enjoyment in sport.

The following story is a wonderful example of how a few sessions of hypnotherapy dramatically changed the life of a local sportsman. He offered to tell his story here.

Case History: Paul Cracknell

I work in the fitness industry and along the way you hear of therapies that come and go, of things that have worked for people and many that haven't. But I'd never met a hypnotherapist before. I'd always wanted to ask them what it's all about, and what it's capable of. To be honest, before talking to Christian, my thoughts on hypnotherapy were that it would be practiced by some eccentric character who would tell me they were going to solve all my problems by rubbing my head!

I first met Christian when he started training at the gym I manage. One day we got chatting. He's an easy-going and approachable guy. I found out he liked his music and that he was a Bowen practitioner. My aunt had been a Bowen therapist so we naturally struck up a conversation. We both liked sport, especially cricket, and that set up some good banter, him being an 'Ozzie' and all! Christian treated my elbow once in the gym using his Bowen technique. I was complaining of tennis elbow and, after a ten-minute session, the next day I was throwing the cricket ball in from the boundary with no problem at all. I was pain-free!

I've always been a motivated character. Setting goals and getting past barriers to succeed are part of my lifestyle and have been for as long as I can remember. I'd call myself an optimistic person and generally would say I'm very confident and outgoing. As a keen sportsman, I naturally seem to have a desire to adapt and achieve. I've never been someone to give up or quit. Instead I try to find different ways to achieve something. I'd say I'm quite open to trying something new if it will help me get to where I want to be.

So when Christian asked me if I'd ever thought of hypnotherapy to help my sports performance, I was pretty happy to give it a go. In my eyes, the worse that could happen was that I'd stay the same.

At the same time, I was also intrigued. Does it really work? How does it work? What potential does it have? I was also excited at the thought of discovering more about myself.

With the cricket season still months away, I decided I wanted to put Christian up to the challenge of improving my sport. I'd say I'm a competent cricketer. I'll usually perform well in a pressure situation and I am fairly confident of my ability in the sport. Before working on the cricket however, I wanted to test Christian out a bit first.

I'm not a keen flyer. I won't let it stop me but I'd love to think I didn't have to consider the various miserable thoughts I've attached to it. 'Damn, I'm going to have to get on a plane for that holiday!' It is quite an annoying anxiety. I haven't always disliked flying, I used to love it, but I had a particularly bumpy episode a few years back that set up my thought processes to avoid flying whenever possible - I can't get out of the plane!

I told Christian about this and asked him if, whilst working on the cricket, would he be able to improve that situation, to make it at least more enjoyable?

He said okay.

I said 'Good, because I'm going on a skiing holiday in a month and I have to fly to get there!'

Christian explained that this might actually help me understand how the method would cross over to sport. He explained the Amygdala to me and how the brain processes thoughts and anxieties. This helped me understand my phobia of flying. It also helped me understand why I might doubt myself on occasion as I walk out to bat in a cricket match.

So we began.

Christian explained we would treat the flying phobia first. It would be done in time to fly for the skiing holiday and it would lead us nicely into the cricket work if it was still required.

My experience with hypnotherapy was very different to how I imagined it would be. It was more of a listening experience that allowed me to understand what was happening in my mind. While I was in a trance I was aware of things that were happening around me. I thought I'd be out for the count, unsure of what had happened but it wasn't like that. I always felt in control. We did three sessions on the flying in total in January 2012.

Since then I've flown more this year than any other time in my life! I flew for the skiing holiday to the Alps, two summer sun holidays including a long flight, and a trip to Ireland for a wedding. The plane to Ireland would have seriously worried me as it was so different to previous larger airline flights. The plane was small with propeller engines, but strangely that didn't really bother me as it would have done in the past.

After returning from my ski holiday, I jumped straight into cricket. My goal setting remained the same, but my attitude towards it was even more confident. Rather than just *thinking* I was good enough to beat other teams, now I *knew* I was. I had always known I had a bigger talent than I was able to show. I knew that if I applied myself I would succeed and achieve my goals. We hadn't even completed a full hypnotherapy session on the sport performance but I knew I was going to have my best season yet. I told Christian that I didn't feel I needed another session specifically on cricket. He understood and was supportive.

Instead we touched base in the gym. I know he is always working his angles during these conversations. We'd finish what seemed like a casual chat and I would always feel more energised and motivated afterwards. In my head I was thinking that if the top batsmen for England can walk in and hit runs week after week against the quality bowling they face, I can do it easily at my club level.

My goals for the season were set:

1. To have my most successful season, measured by runs scored and batting average.
2. To establish myself as a top order Batsman, possibly 3rd or 4th in.
3. To win the 'Player of the Year' award.
4. To win the 'Fastest 50' trophy.
5. To hit a significant score for the First team.

I enjoyed batting for the first time in years and I felt totally relaxed at the crease. The bowling attacks couldn't throw down a ball that I felt was good enough to get me out and it showed with my scoring.

In a particularly hard game, I asked our captain to put me in at three when we had a high run chase. I'd never do this normally but I was feeling so confident and I saw my opportunity to achieve my second goal. As cocky as he thought I was, the captain gave me a shot. The only way we'd have a chance of winning would be if we scored quickly so I went for it. I hit 96 runs in 20 overs. This gave us a real chance of winning that game and it cemented me as the number 3 batsman for the rest of the season.

However, my most memorable moment from the season 2012 saw me come in with 6 runs needed to win from the last 3 balls of a very tight game. It was a real pressure situation. I was facing their fastest opening bowler who had come on to clean up our tail end. The first ball I lobbed back over the bowler for 2 runs. This kept me on strike. 4 runs from 2 balls needed. The field was set deep, expecting the big shot to get the four runs needed.

My thought process did exactly the following: 'Relax. This is what you play for. You know what this bowler is going to do. It's going to be quick, straight and full. He isn't going to risk anything fancy as he could lose them the game. There is a big crowd watching and they are going to go mental when you hit him straight over his head for six, over the sight screen. If you hit a big one, you won't get caught and the crowd will love the audacity you have shown to not just go for two small hits, or even a four, but for the big win. You need to take two steps out of your crease to meet the ball on the half volley so you can punch it hard. You've hit so many sixes like this. Winning the game on this next delivery is the moment. There will be more pressure if you have another ball to face. Oh, and remember to celebrate. This win means something!'

Just like with the flying, I'd already run through what was going to happen, practicing it in my head.

The bowler runs in. Fast. The ball comes down. Full and straight. I stepped forward to meet the ball on the half volley. I hit it hard. In the sweet spot of the bat. I watched it launch over the bowler's head, straight over the sight screen, out of the ground and into a hedge. Cue cheering crowd. I celebrate down onto one knee in the middle of the pitch, punching the air to the crowd. We won the game. I can honestly say it was more satisfying hitting those eight runs than any 50 or 100 I've ever hit!

I let Christian know throughout the season how well things were going.

In the season of 2012 I scored:

98, 96, 74*, 70, 64, 49*, 44* (*not out)

- I achieved every goal I set this year:
- I scored the most runs I've ever scored in a season.
- I nearly doubled my highest average ever.
- I batted at number 3 for most of the season.
- I was voted Second Team 'Player of the Year' by my teammates.
- I won the 'Fastest 50' trophy, scoring 98 against Nailsea.
- I scored 44 Not Out and 70 for the First Team when I finally got my opportunities.
- I finished the season as second highest run scorer, with the second highest average for my club.
- I was second only to our club captain who is the most outstanding cricketer I've ever played with or against.

Next year, I've asked Christian to do some more work with me on my sport. I feel I can do even better again. I set my goals in the New Year for the year ahead. I write them down and evaluate the previous year's success, and I look forward to what I need to do for the next season. Once that's done I'll be back on the couch!

I can see now how hypnotherapy helps people. You don't have to be a certain type of person, or have a certain personality to do it. You just have to really want to sort out those issues that you'd like to change.

Paul Cracknell

What's Been Good About Your Day?

Write down a list of 3 things that have been GOOD about your day, no matter how small or insignificant you might think them to be. Feel free to write more if you want to.

1. _____

   _____

2. _____

   _____

3. _____

   _____

Now listen to the MP3.

Congratulations...

You made that commitment to start something new and you followed through on that commitment. Making real changes in your life.

By following this program and reading through the processes and experiences shared in this book over the last 30 days you have become consciously aware of how your mind creates your world. Developing and using new resources. Harnessing the physical power of neuroplasticity to create new pathways for thinking in your brain.

Remember, habits are created through repetition. By keeping a daily record, a journal or diary of what has been good about your day, you have created the habit of gratitude - being grateful for the good things that happen. Opening up your awareness of the little things, those seemingly simple events that bring you joy and happiness daily. You've also trained your mind to start operating from the Left Prefrontal Cortex area of our brain. That creative part that tends to get things right, where we come up with solutions.

Listening to the MP3 every night has focused the subconscious mind and the conscious mind on the positive suggestions and influences that help unscramble the mixed messages in our mind. Through deep relaxation you have been letting go of stress, creating the space in your mind that opens up new opportunities and possibilities, and seeing those possibilities clearly, motivating you to move forward positively.

And all the time over the last 30 days, that wonderful neurotransmitter serotonin has been flowing, helping you to cope in a calm, relaxed way with the events that make up your life.

So what next?

Keep going. I highly recommend you keep doing what works. Just as going to the gym helps you stay physically fit and healthy, feel motivated and energised, so you keep going.

Writing down what's been good about your day in a journal or notebook, and listening to the MP3 helps you stay focused and positive, calm and relaxed – so keep doing it. Make the most of the resources available to you.

You can go to my website and download my free MP3 for Mindfulness. Starting a short daily practice using my Mindfulness MP3 is a powerful addition to the positive resources available to you.

Share your experience with others. Your positive experiences not only become what's been good about your day, they inspire family, friends and colleagues to appreciate the positive things in their own lives... and the ripples spread.

If you want to take your progress to another level, I highly recommend having a talk to a Solution Focused Hypnotherapist. It costs nothing for an initial consultation. I see people at my clinic in the Sunshine Coast Hinterland, Australia, and all over the world via Skype. Or you can contact the Association for Solution Focused Hypnotherapists at www.afsfh.co.uk to find a therapist near you. One-to-one sessions with a qualified Solution Focused Hypnotherapist can help resolve long-established phobias, lower anxiety, and help lift depression quickly. There is no need to suffer in silence.

These resources are yours now. You have taken control of your thoughts and how you think. This gives you control of your feelings, and ultimately what you do or don't do.

Take those next steps that are best for you. Move forward confidently, knowing that you are in control. Clear, calm and confident.

Take your time.

Enjoy every step of your journey... and keep going.

www.christiandunham.net

Further reading

'A User's Guide To The Brain'
John Ratey

'The Human Givens'
Joe Griffin & Ivan Tyrrell

'The Divided Mind'
John E. Sarno M.D.

'The Joy Of Living'
Yongey Mingyur Rinpoche

Association For Solution Focused Hypnotherapists (AfSFH)

www.afsfh.co.uk